The instructions and answer grid for completion of Section 1 in each practice from **www.hoddereducation.co.uk/updatesandextras**

Higher
Human
Biology
Practice Papers for SQA Exams

Billy Dickson

Graham Moffat

Contents

West Lothian Council

3 8053 02186 059 3

HODDER GIBSON
AN HACHETTE UK COMPANY

The Publishers would like to thank the following for permission to reproduce copyright material:

Acknowledgements

Exam rubric in Section 1 and Section 2 of each practice paper; online instructions and marking grid for completion of Section 1, Copyright © Scottish Qualifications Authority

Every effort has been made to trace all copyright holders, but if any have been inadvertently overlooked the Publishers will be pleased to make the necessary arrangements at the first opportunity.

Although every effort has been made to ensure that website addresses are correct at time of going to press, Hodder Gibson cannot be held responsible for the content of any website mentioned in this book. It is sometimes possible to find a relocated web page by typing in the address of the home page for a website in the URL window of your browser.

Hachette UK's policy is to use papers that are natural, renewable and recyclable products and made from wood grown in sustainable forests. The logging and manufacturing processes are expected to conform to the environmental regulations of the country of origin.

Orders: please contact Bookpoint Ltd, 130 Park Drive, Milton Park, Abingdon, Oxon OX14 4SE. Telephone: (44) 01235 827720. Fax: (44) 01235 400454. Lines are open 9.00–5.00, Monday to Saturday, with a 24-hour message answering service. Visit our website at www.hoddereducation.co.uk. Hodder Gibson can be contacted direct on: Tel: 0141 333 4650; Fax: 0141 404 8188; email: hoddergibson@hodder.co.uk

© Billy Dickson, Graham Moffat 2017

First published in 2017 by
Hodder Gibson, an imprint of Hodder Education,
An Hachette UK Company
211 St Vincent Street
Glasgow G2 5QY

Impression number	5 4 3 2 1
Year	2021 2020 2019 2018 2017

All rights reserved. Apart from any use permitted under UK copyright law, no part of this publication may be reproduced or transmitted in any form or by any means, electronic or mechanical, including photocopying and recording, or held within any information storage and retrieval system, without permission in writing from the publisher or under licence from the Copyright Licensing Agency Limited. Further details of such licences (for reprographic reproduction) may be obtained from the Copyright Licensing Agency Limited, www.cla.co.uk

Cover photo © Sebastian Kaulitzki/123RF.com
Illustrations by Aptara, Inc.
Typeset in Din regular, 12/14.4 pts. by Aptara, Inc.
Printed in the UK

A catalogue record for this title is available from the British Library

ISBN: 978 1 5104 1502 7

Introduction

Higher Human Biology

The three papers included in this book are designed to provide practice and to support revision for the Higher Human Biology course assessment question paper (the examination), which is worth 83% of the final grade for this course.

Together, the three papers give overall and comprehensive coverage of Demonstrating and Applying Knowledge and the Skills of Scientific Inquiry needed to pass Higher Human Biology.

Design of the papers

Each paper has been carefully assembled to be very similar to a typical Higher Human Biology question paper. Each paper has 100 marks and is divided into two sections.

Section 1 – Objective Test, which contains 20 multiple choice items worth 1 mark each and totalling 20 marks altogether.

Section 2 – Paper 2, which contains restricted and extended response questions. There are two extended writing questions in each paper, worth 10–15 marks in total. The extended writing questions include a choice of topic. Each paper has a large data-handling question and a large experimental design question.

In each paper, the marks are distributed proportionately across all four component units of the course and in each paper 65–75 marks are for Demonstrating and Applying knowledge. The remaining 25–35 marks are for the application of Skills of Scientific Inquiry. We have included features of the National Papers, such as offering choice in some questions.

70% of the marks in each paper are set at the standard of Grade C and the remaining 30% are more difficult marks set at the standard for Grade A. We have attempted to construct each paper to represent the typical range of demand in a Higher Human Biology paper.

Key Area index grids

The **Key Area index grids** on pages vii–xii show the pattern of coverage of the knowledge in the Key Areas and the Skills across the three papers. We have provided marks totals for each Key Area and Skill. Scoring more than half of these marks suggests that you have a good grasp of the content of that specific Key Area or Skill.

After having worked on questions from a particular Key Area or Skill, you might want to use the traffic light boxes to show progress – red for 'not understood', orange for 'more work needed', and green for 'fully understood'. If you continue to struggle with a set of Key Area or Skills questions, you should see you teacher for extra help.

Student Margins

The question pages have Student Margins in which we have cross referenced each question to the Course Assessment Specification (CAS) from the SQA website at www.sqa.org.uk and to the appropriate 'Key Points' pages in Hodder Gibson's *How to Pass Higher Human Biology* (HTP). The margins also have a key to each question to show what is being tested and the level of demand intended, as shown in the table below. For questions worth more than 1 mark, we have allocated each mark to a demand level. For example, **CA** means 1 mark at **C** and the second at **A**. For questions testing Skills, we have referenced to the Skills of Scientific Inquiry chapter of *How to Pass*, although the CAS reference is for the Key Area from which the question context was taken.

Key	Meaning
dKU	Demonstrating knowledge and understanding of biology
aKU	Applying knowledge of biology to new situations, interpreting information and solving problems
Planning	Planning or designing experiments to test given hypotheses
Selecting	Selecting information from a variety of sources
Presenting	Presenting information appropriately in a variety of forms
Processing	Processing information using calculations and units where appropriate
Predicting	Making predictions and generalisations based on evidence
Concluding	Drawing valid conclusions and giving explanations supported by evidence
Evaluating	Evaluating experiments and investigations and suggesting improvements
C	Basic level of demand linked with Grade C
A	More challenging level of demand linked with Grade A

Using the Papers

Each Paper can be attempted or groups of questions on a particular Key Area or Skill can be tackled – use the Key Area index grid to find related groups of questions. In the grid, questions have been allocated to the main area being tested. Use the Date Completed column to keep a record of your progress.

We recommend working between attempting the questions and studying the answers (see below). You will find a reference to the location of the answers at the end of each Objective Test and following each Section 2 question.

Where any difficulty is encountered, it is worth trying to consolidate by reading the referenced material from *How to Pass*. Use the information in the Student Margin to identify the type of question you find most tricky. Be aware that Grade A-type questions are expected to be challenging.

You will need a pen, sharp pencil, clear plastic ruler and a calculator for the best results. A couple of different coloured highlighters could also be handy.

Using the Extended Response Question Practice

Extended response questions are worth between 10 and 15 marks in each question paper and so can make a big difference to your grade for the exam. We have given 36 extended responses with varied mark allocations and ranging across the whole course. Each is referenced to its Key Area in the Course Assessment Specification (CAS) and the 'Key Points' pages in *How to Pass* (HTP). Preparing well by practising with these questions and marking your own work using the model answers on pages 148–164 is essential. To boost your confidence, it is a nice idea to have answers to a few extended response questions for each Unit stored solidly in your memory! There is a grid on page xii in which you can record your progress with extended response questions.

Answers

The expected answers on pages 120–147 give National Standard answers but, occasionally, there may be other acceptable answers. There is a commentary with hints and tips provided alongside each answer. Don't feel you need to use them all!

The commentaries on the answers focus on the biology itself as well as giving hints and tips, a focus on traditionally difficult areas, advice on wording of answers, and notes of common errors.

Grading

The three papers are designed to be equally demanding and to reflect the National Standard of a typical SQA paper. Each paper has 100 marks – if you score 50 marks that is a C pass. You will need about 60 marks for a B pass and about 70 marks for an A. These figures are a rough guide only.

Timing

If you are attempting a full paper, limit yourself to **two hours and thirty minutes** to complete. Get someone to time you! We recommend no more than 25 minutes for the Objective Test and the remainder of the time for Section 2.

If you are tackling blocks of questions in a Key Area or Skill, give yourself about a minute and a half per mark; for example, a set of questions worth 10 marks should take about 15 minutes.

Key Area calendar

You could use the Key Area calendar below to plan revision for your final exam. There are 24 Key Areas, so covering two each week would require a 12-week revision programme. The exams are in May, so starting after your February holiday would give you time – just!

Key Area revised	Date	Questions completed (✓)	Green light for confidence! (✓)
1.1 Division and differentiation in human cells			
1.2 Structure and replication of DNA			
1.3 Gene expression			
1.4 Genes and proteins in health and disease			
1.5 Human genomics			
1.6 Metabolic pathways			
1.7 Cellular respiration			
1.8 Energy systems in muscle cells			

Key Area revised	Date	Questions completed (✔)	Green light for confidence! (✔)
2.1 The structure and function of reproductive organs and gametes and their role in fertilisation			
2.2 Hormonal control of reproduction			
2.3 The biology of controlling fertility			
2.4 Ante- and postnatal screening			
2.5 The structure and function of arteries, capillaries and veins			
2.6 The structure and function of the heart			
2.7 Pathology of cardiovascular disease			
2.8 Blood glucose levels and obesity			
3.1 Divisions of the nervous system and parts of the brain			
3.2 Perception and memory			
3.3 The cells of the nervous system and neurotransmitters at synapses			
3.4 Communication and social behaviour			
4.1 Non-specific defences			
4.2 Specific cellular defences			
4.3 The transmission and control of infectious disease			
4.4 Active immunisation and vaccination, and the evasion of specific immune responses by pathogens			

Good luck!

Key Area index grids

Core Units

Skill tested	Key Area	Practice Paper Questions, (OT – Objective Test; P2 – Paper 2)			Mark	Traffic light	Date completed
		Paper 1	**Paper 2**	**Paper 3**			
Demonstrating and Applying Knowledge — Unit 1 Human Cells	1.1 Division and differentiation in human cells	**OT** Q3 **P2** Q1	**OT** Q1 **P2** Q3	**OT** Q4 **P2** Q1	/16		
	1.2 Structure and replication of DNA	**OT** Q1,2 **P2** –	**OT** – **P2** Q1	**OT** – **P2** Q14A	/15		
	1.3 Gene expression	**OT** Q4 **P2** Q2	**OT** Q5 **P2** –	**OT** Q2 **P2** Q2	/13		
	1.4 Genes and proteins in health and disease	**OT** – **P2** Q3	**OT** Q4 **P2** –	**OT** Q3 **P2** –	/6		
	1.5 Human genomics	**OT** Q5 **P2** –	**OT** – **P2** Q2ai,iii,b,c	**OT** – **P2** Q4	/9		
	1.6 Metabolic pathways	**OT** Q7,10 **P2** Q4	**OT** Q3 **P2** –	**OT** Q5 **P2** Q14B	/17		
	1.7 Cellular respiration	**OT** – **P2** –	**OT** – **P2** Q5	**OT** – **P2** Q3ai,ii,iii	/10		
	1.8 Energy systems in muscle cells	**OT** – **P2** Q5aiv,bii	**OT** Q6 **P2** –	**OT** – **P2** Q3aiv	/6		

Skill tested	Key Area	Practice Paper Questions (OT – Objective Test; P2 – Paper 2)			Marks	Traffic light	Date completed
Unit 2 Physiology and Health Demonstrating and Applying Knowledge	2.1 The structure and function of reproductive organs and gametes and their role in fertilisation	**OT** Q8 **P2** –	**OT** – **P2** Q7b,c	**OT** – **P2** –	/4		
	2.2 Hormonal control of reproduction	**OT** – **P2** Q6	**OT** – **P2** Q7a	**OT** Q8,12 **P2** –	/9		
	2.3 The biology of controlling fertility	**OT** – **P2** –	**OT** – **P2** Q14A	**OT** Q9 **P2** –	/9		
	2.4 Ante- and postnatal screening	**OT** – **P2** Q7	**OT** Q8,14 **P2** Q14B	**OT** Q13 **P2** –	/16		
	2.5 The structure and function of arteries, capillaries and veins	**OT** Q11,12 **P2** –	**OT** – **P2** Q6e	**OT** – **P2** Q5a,b	/6		
	2.6 The structure and function of the heart	**OT** – **P2** Q10	**OT** – **P2** Q6b	**OT** Q10 **P2** –	/7		
	2.7 Pathology of cardiovascular disease	**OT** – **P2** Q9	**OT** Q11 **P2** –	**OT** – **P2** Q5c	/7		
	2.8 Blood glucose levels and obesity	**OT** – **P2** Q8b	**OT** Q13 **P2** –	**OT** – **P2** Q6b,c	/6		

Higher Human Biology

Skill tested	Key Area	Practice Paper Questions (OT – Objective Test; P2 – Paper 2)			Marks	Traffic light	Date completed
Unit 3 **Neurobiology and Communication** Demonstrating and Applying Knowledge	3.1 Divisions of the nervous system and parts of the brain	**OT** Q14 **P2** Q11	**OT** – **P2** Q9ai, ii	**OT** Q16 **P2** –	/8		
	3.2 Perception and memory	**OT** Q15,17 **P2** –	**OT** – **P2** Q9aiii,b	**OT** – **P2** Q8	/8		
	3.3 The cells of the nervous system and neurotransmitters at synapses	**OT** – **P2** Q12	**OT** Q15,16 **P2** Q11	**OT** Q15 **P2** –	/15		
	3.4 Communication and social behaviour	**OT** Q16 **P2** –	**OT** – **P2** Q10	**OT** – **P2** Q10	/10		

Skill tested	Key Area	Practice Paper Questions (OT – Objective Test; P2 – Paper 2)			Marks	Traffic light	Date completed
Unit 4 Immunology and Public Health Demonstrating and Applying Knowledge	4.1 Non-specific defences	**OT** – **P2** Q15A	**OT** – **P2** –	**OT** – **P2** Q7, 11b	/14		
	4.2 Specific cellular defences	**OT** – **P2** Q15B	**OT** Q19 **P2** Q12a,b	**OT** – **P2** Q11a	/17		
	4.3 The transmission and control of infectious disease	**OT** – **P2** Q14bi	**OT** Q20 **P2** –	**OT** – **P2** Q13	/6		
	4.4 Active immunisation and vaccination, and the evasion of specific immune responses by pathogens	**OT** Q19 **P2** –	**OT** – **P2** Q6a	**OT** Q18,19 **P2** –	/5		

Skill tested	Key Area	Practice Paper Questions (OT – Objective Test; P2 – Paper 2)			Marks	Traffic light	Date completed
Human Biology Course — Skills of Scientific Inquiry	Planning	**OT** – **P2** Q13a,b,c	**OT** – **P2** Q4a,b,c,d	**OT** Q7 **P2** Q12b,c	/14		
	Selecting	**OT** Q6,18 **P2** Q5ai,iii,bi, 8a,14ai	**OT** Q2,7,10,12 **P2** Q2aii,6c,8a, 13aiii,b	**OT** Q14 **P2** Q3bi,6a,9aiii,c	/29		
	Presenting	**OT** – **P2** Q13di	**OT** – **P2** Q4e	**OT** – **P2** Q12d	/7		
	Processing	**OT** Q9,13,20 **P2** Q5aii,14aii	**OT** Q9,18 **P2** Q13ai,ii,c	**OT** Q1,11 **P2** Q3bii, 9ai,ii,b,12a	/17		
	Predicting	**OT** – **P2** Q14bii	**OT** – **P2** Q8c	**OT** – **P2** Q9aiv	/3		
	Concluding	**OT** – **P2** Q13dii	**OT** Q17 **P2** Q4f,6d,12bi,ii	**OT** Q6,17,20 **P2** Q12ei	/12		
	Evaluating	**OT** – **P2** Q13diii	**OT** – **P2** Q8b	**OT** – **P2** Q12eii	/4		
Marks totals		100	100	100	300		

Extended Response Questions

Unit	Key Area	Question	Mark	Secure (✓)	More work needed (✓)
Unit 1 Human Cells	1.1	1	/8		
	1.2	2	/9		
	1.3	3	/8		
	1.4	4	/7		
	1.4	5	/6		
	1.5	6	/6		
	1.6	7	/10		
	1.6	8	/9		
	1.7	9	/9		
	1.7	10	/8		
	1.7	11	/8		
	1.8	12	/6		
	1.8	13	/10		
Total for Unit 1			**/104**		
Unit 2 Physiology and Health	2.1	14	/8		
	2.2	15	/6		
	2.2	16	/9		
	2.2	17	/9		
	2.2	18	/10		
	2.3	19	/9		
	2.4	20	/9		
	2.5	21	/9		
	2.6	22	/10		
	2.7	23	/6		
	2.8	24	/9		
Total for Unit 2			**/94**		
Unit 3 Neurobiology	3.1	25	/8		
	3.2	26	/9		
	3.3	27	/8		
	3.3	28	/9		
	3.4	29	/7		
	3.4	30	/6		
Total for Unit 3			**/47**		
Unit 4 Immunology	4.1	31	/9		
	4.2	32	/7		
	4.2	33	/7		
	4.3	34	/6		
	4.3	35	/9		
	4.4	36	/7		
Total for Unit 4			**/45**		
Overall ER Total			**/290**		

Higher Human Biology

HODDER
GIBSON
LEARN MORE

Duration – 2 hours and 30 minutes

Total marks – 100

SECTION 1 – 20 marks

Attempt ALL questions.

SECTION 2 – 80 marks

Attempt ALL questions.

Question 15 contains a choice.

Write your answers clearly in the spaces provided in this paper. Additional space for answers and rough work is provided at the end of this paper. If you use this space, you must clearly identify the question number you are attempting. Any rough work must be written in this paper. You should score through your rough work when you have written your final copy.

Use **blue** or **black** ink.

Section 1

SECTION 1 – 20 MARKS

Attempt ALL questions. Answer grid available at www.hoddereducation.co.uk/updatesandextras.

STUDENT MARGIN

1   Which of the following diagrams shows how the strands of a DNA molecule are arranged?

A

B

C

D

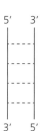

CAS
KA 1.2
Page 9

HTP
Page 10

dKU
C

2   If 10% of the bases in a molecule of DNA are cytosine, what is the ratio of cytosine to thymine in the same molecule?

   A 1 : 1

   B 1 : 2

   C 1 : 3

   D 1 : 4

CAS
KA 1.2
Page 9

HTP
Page 10

aKU
C

3 The diagram below shows a parent skin cell containing DNA molecules in its nucleus. After two rounds of cell division, how many daughter cells would contain an original strand of a DNA molecule found in the parent skin cell?

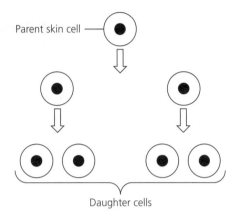

Parent skin cell

Daughter cells

CAS
KA 1.1
Page 8

HTP
Page 1

aKU
A

A 1
B 2
C 4
D 8

4 The diagram below represents a stage in protein synthesis in a cell.

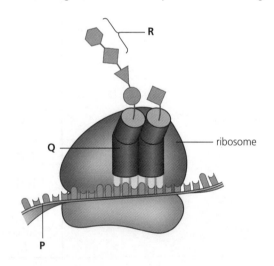

R

Q

ribosome

P

CAS
KA 1.3
Page 9

HTP
Page 16

dKU
C

Which line in the table below identifies molecules P, Q and R?

	Molecules		
	P	**Q**	**R**
A	tRNA	mRNA	Peptide
B	mRNA	Peptide	tRNA
C	mRNA	tRNA	Peptide
D	tRNA	Peptide	mRNA

5 The graph below shows the temperature changes involved in one thermal cycle of the polymerase chain reaction (PCR).

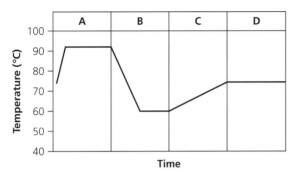

Which letter indicates a region in which DNA polymerase would be most active?

CAS
KA 1.5
Page 10

HTP
Page 29

dKU
C

6 The graph below shows the effect of substrate concentration on the rate of an enzyme-catalysed reaction.

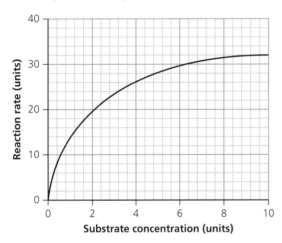

At which substrate concentration is the reaction rate equal to 75% of the maximum rate?

A   2.6
B   3.2
C   6.4
D   7.5

CAS
KA 1.6
Page 10

HTP
Page 35

Selecting
A

7 In a metabolic pathway, feedback inhibition can occur when its:

A   end product binds to a substrate involved in an earlier step in the pathway

B   final enzyme binds to a substrate involved in an earlier step in the pathway

C   end product binds to an enzyme involved in an earlier step in the pathway

D   final enzyme binds to a product of an earlier step in the pathway.

CAS
KA 1.6
Page 10

HTP
Page 35

dKU
C

8 The diagram below shows a section through seminiferous tubules in the testes.

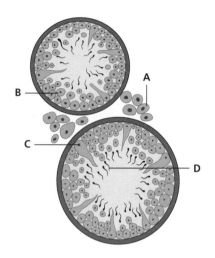

CAS
KA 2.1
Page 11

HTP
Page 64

dKU
C

Which letter indicates a target cell for the hormone ICSH?

9 As part of an investigation into human fertility, mean sperm counts were made from semen samples of groups of men over the period between 1940 and 2000.

The results are shown on the graph below.

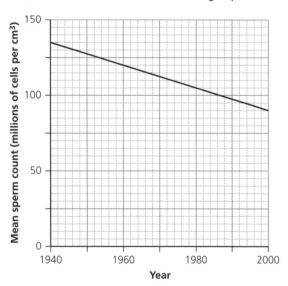

CAS
KA 2.1
Page 11

HTP
Page 64

Processing
A

What is the average reduction in mean sperm count per year over the period of the study?

A 0.67 million per cm³

B 0.75 million per cm³

C 0.92 million per cm³

D 45 million per cm³

10 Alcaptonuria is a disorder in which a metabolic block causes a failure to produce the enzyme that catalyses the breakdown of homogentisate into maleylacetoacetate, as shown in the metabolic pathway below.

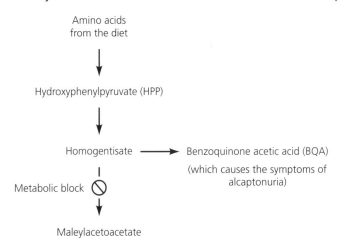

From the information given, which row in the table below shows the likely effect of this metabolic block on the concentration of the substances shown?

	Increased concentration	Decreased concentration
A	BQA only	Maleylacetoacetate only
B	HPP and homogentisate	Maleylacetoacetate only
C	BQA and homogentisate	HPP and homogentisate
D	BQA only	Homogentisate and BQA

11 Which of the diagrams below best represents a cross-section through an artery?

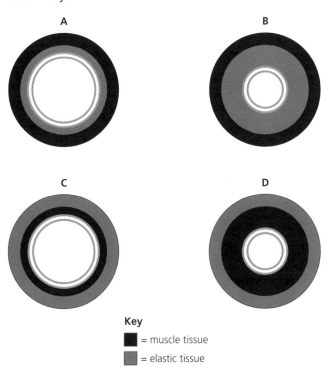

Key
■ = muscle tissue
▦ = elastic tissue

CAS
KA 1.6
Page 10

HTP
Page 35

aKU
C

CAS
KA 2.5
Page 12

HTP
Page 91

aKU
C

12 The diagram below shows the relationship between blood capillaries, body cells and lymph capillaries.

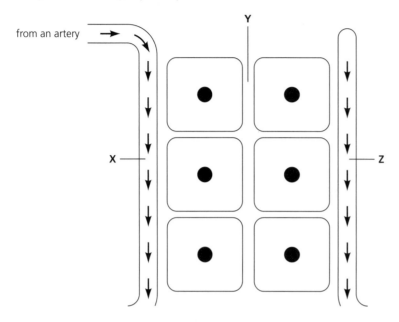

from an artery →

Y

X

Z

CAS
KA 2.5
Page 12

HTP
Page 91

aKU
C

In which region(s) of the diagram would plasma protein molecules be found?

A   X only

B   X and Y

C   Y and Z

D   Z only

13 Mean arterial pressure (MAP) is a measure of blood pressure in arteries.
Pulse pressure is the difference between systolic and diastolic blood pressure.
MAP is calculated using the formula:

$$\text{MAP} = \text{diastolic pressure} + \left(\frac{\text{pulse pressure}}{3} \right)$$

What is the MAP of an individual with a blood pressure reading of 120/75 mmHg?

A   90 mmHg

B   120 mmHg

C   135 mmHg

D   165 mmHg

CAS
KA 2.6
Page 12

HTP
Page 97

Processing
A

14 Which line in the table below identifies actions of branches in the autonomic nervous system?

	Parasympathetic	Sympathetic
A	Heart rate increased	Heart rate decreased
B	Increased release of saliva	Decreased release of saliva
C	Decreased rate of peristalsis	Increased rate of peristalsis
D	Increased breathing rate	Decreased breathing rate

CAS
KA 3.1
Page 13

HTP
Page 135

dKU
C

15 Perceptual set influences how an individual perceives an image. Individuals may perceive the image below as an ornamental vase or as the outlines of two faces looking at each other.

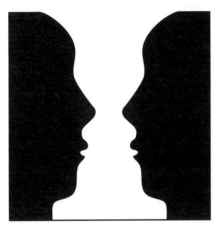

Which of the following is **not** likely to play a part in formation of the perceptual set of the individuals in this case?

A Previous experience

B Binocular disparity

C Context

D Expectation

CAS
KA 3.2
Page 14

HTP
Page 140

aKU
C

16 A young child is scratched by a cat. After this experience, she shows fear of all cats.

This type of behaviour is called:

A shaping

B internalisation

C discrimination

D generalisation.

CAS
KA 3.4
Page 15

HTP
Page 158

aKU
C

17 The diagram below shows features of the relationship between short- and long-term memory.

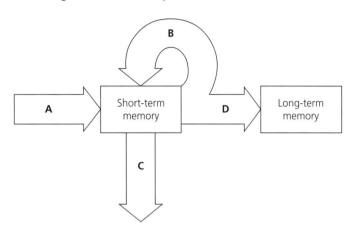

Which arrow could represent the process of displacement?

CAS
KA 3.2
Page 14

HTP
Page 140

aKU
C

18 Acquired immune deficiency syndrome (AIDS) is a condition which may develop from an HIV infection. The graph below shows the numbers in the world population infected by HIV and the numbers of deaths from AIDS between 1990 and 2010.

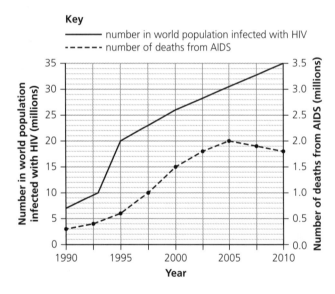

During the year in which 1 million people died from AIDS, how many millions of people were infected with HIV?

A 1.8

B 10

C 23

D 26

CAS
KA 4.3
Page 16

HTP
Page 181

Selecting
A

19 Adjuvants are often added to vaccines to:

A   make the vaccines safer

B   enhance the immune response that the vaccines trigger

C   make the immunity that the vaccines produce last longer

D   ensure total removal of pathogens from the vaccines.

CAS
KA 4.4
Page 16
HTP
Page 184
dKU
C

20 The graphs below show the effects of two injections of an antigen on the concentrations of the antibody produced against it in the blood of a patient.

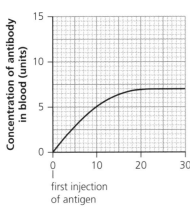
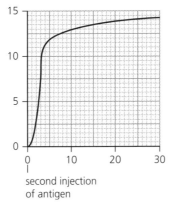

Time (days)

What is the percentage increase in the concentration of antibodies in the blood of the patient 10 days after the second injection compared to 10 days after the first?

A   38

B   62.5

C   160

D   260

CAS
KA 4.2
Page 16

HTP
Page 175

Processing
A

[End of Section 1 – Answers on page 120–121]

[Now attempt the questions in Section 2]

Section 2

SECTION 2 – 80 marks

Attempt ALL questions.

Question 15 contains a choice.

Write your answers clearly in the spaces provided in this paper. Additional space for answers and rough work is provided at the end of this paper. If you use this space you must clearly identify the question number you are attempting. Any rough work must be written in this space. You should score through your rough work when you have written your final copy.

Use **blue** or **black** ink.

MARKS   STUDENT MARGIN

1 The diagram below shows the role of embryonic stem cells in the development of a human embryo.

Early human embryo

Embryonic stem cells

Cells with specialised functions in later embryo

CAS
KA 1.1
Page 8

HTP
Page 1

a) Give the term used to describe the process by which a cell develops specialised functions.

1   dKU C

b) Describe one way in which tissue (adult) stem cells differ from embryonic stem cells.

1   dKU C

	MARKS	STUDENT MARGIN

c) Describe how cancer cells form a tumour and explain how secondary tumours can arise.

Description _____ **1**

_____

Explanation _____ **1**

_____

dKU
CA

[Model answers on page 122]

STUDENT
MARKS   MARGIN

2   The diagram below shows part of a DNA template strand and a
part of a primary RNA transcript synthesised from it.

X

DNA template   3'   5'

Primary RNA transcript

exon   intron

		CAS **KA** 1.3 Page 9 **HTP** Page 16

a)   Give the term used to describe the process shown in
the diagram.   1

_____

b)   DNA is encoded in triplet sequences.
Explain what is meant by this.   1

_____

_____

c) **(i)**   Name the enzyme responsible for synthesising the
primary RNA transcript.   1

_____

(ii)   Describe a possible effect on the primary RNA transcript
of a single nucleotide mutation at point X on the DNA template.   1

_____

_____

_____

1	aKU C
1	dKU C
1	dKU C
1	aKU A

[Model answers on page 122]

3 The table below shows single nucleotide substitution mutations of human genes and the possible effect they may have.

a) Complete the table by adding correct information to the empty boxes.

Name of single nucleotide substitution	Possible effect of the mutation on the protein synthesised
	A correct amino acid replaced by an incorrect one in a polypeptide chain
Nonsense	

b) One form of Down syndrome (DS) is caused by a translocation mutation that produces substantial changes to an affected individual's genetic material.

(i) Describe what is meant by translocation.

_____

_____

(ii) Apart from translocation, name **one other** type of mutation that can affect the structure of human chromosomes.

_____

2

1

1

CAS
KA 1.4
Page 9
HTP
Page 23

dKU
CA

dKU
C

dKU
C

[Model answers on page 122]

4 The diagram below represents molecules involved in an enzyme-catalysed reaction in the presence of an inhibitor.

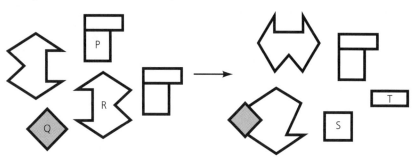

a) Use letters from the diagram to identify an inhibitor molecule and a substrate molecule.

Molecule	Letter from diagram
Inhibitor	
Substrate	

b) Name the type of inhibition occurring in this example and explain how the inhibitor molecules produce their effect.

Type of inhibition_____

Explanation_____

_____

CAS
KA 1.6
Page 10

HTP
Page 35

2

dKU
CC

2

dKU
CA

[Model answers on page 123]

5 During strenuous exercise, the following processes occur in muscle cells.
- Creatine phosphate is broken down to release energy and phosphate, which are used to produce ATP as shown on the diagram below.

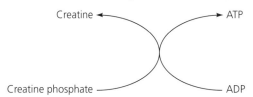

- Pyruvate is converted to lactic acid when oxygen becomes deficient.

The graph below shows the concentrations of creatine phosphate and lactic acid in the muscle cells of a middle-distance runner over a 20 second period on a treadmill, during which he jogged gently for the first 10 seconds then sprinted strenuously for 10 seconds.

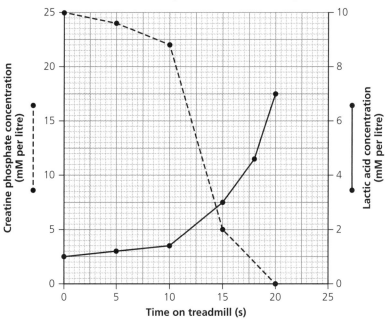

a) **(i)** Give the lactic acid concentration in muscle cells after 15 seconds.

_____mM per litre   **1**

(ii) Calculate the average increase in lactic acid concentration per second over the total 20 seconds.

Space for calculation

_____mM per litre   **1**

STUDENT
MARKS   MARGIN

(iii) Give the creatine phosphate concentration when the
lactic acid concentration was 5 mM per litre.

_____mM per litre   1

Selecting
A

(iv) Explain the reasons for the changes in concentration of
the two substances shown in the graph.

Creatine phosphate _____   1

_____

_____

Lactic acid _____   1

aKU
AA

_____

_____

b) The chart below shows the percentages of fast and slow
twitch muscle fibres in the muscles of a middle-distance
runner compared with those of athletes in other categories and
in untrained individuals.

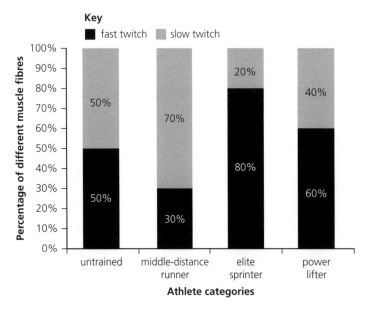

	MARKS	STUDENT MARGIN

(i) Describe the differences in the percentages of muscle types in the middle-distance runner compared with:

an untrained individual _____ **1**

_____

an elite sprinter _____ **1**

_____

(ii) Explain how the percentages of the different fibres found in the muscles of power lifters are suitable for their activity. **1**

_____

_____

Selecting
CC

aKU
A

[Model answers on pages 123–124]

STUDENT
MARKS   MARGIN

6 The graph below shows the relative concentrations of three hormones in the blood plasma of a woman during a 28-day menstrual cycle.

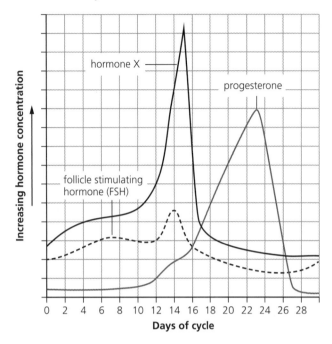

CAS
KA 2.2
Page 11

HTP
Page 68

a) Name hormone X, which triggers ovulation.

1

aKU
C

_____

b) Describe the effects of progesterone on the uterus as it:

(i) increases in concentration from about day 12;

1

dKU
C

_____

_____

(ii) decreases in concentration after day 23.

1

dKU
C

_____

_____

c) Name the gland which releases follicle stimulating hormone (FSH) and describe the role of FSH in fertility.

2

Name_____

Role in fertility_____

dKU
CC

_____

_____

[Model answers on page 124]

7 The pedigree chart below shows the inheritance of haemophilia in a family.

The allele for haemophilia (h) is sex-linked and recessive to the normal allele (H).

Key
☐ male without the condition
■ male with the condition
○ female without the condition
● female with the condition

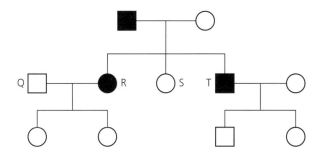

a) (i) Explain why individual R has haemophili a even although her mother was not affected.

_____

_____

1	aKU A

(ii) Give the genotype of individual S.

_____

1	aKU A

b) Individuals Q and R are expecting their third child.

Following the results of an amniocentesis test, the parents are told that their expected baby will be male.

(i) Describe what is meant by an amniocentesis test and explain how the test can reveal the gender of an unborn baby.

Meaning _____

_____

1	dKU C

Explanation _____

_____

_____

1	aKU A

MARKS

(ii) Calculate the percentage chance that the expected male baby of individuals Q and R will have haemophilia.

Space for calculation

1

aKU
A

_____%

[Model answers on pages 124–125]

8   Gastric band surgery (GBS) can be used to treat individuals with obesity. In a clinical trial, sensitivity to insulin was measured in groups of GBS patients with and without type 2 diabetes. In type 2 diabetes, liver cell sensitivity to insulin is low.

The patients' sensitivity to insulin was measured before and after the GBS procedure. The mean results as well as the ranges of values obtained in the trial are shown in the table below.

The higher the number of units, the greater the sensitivity to insulin.

Patient group	Mean insulin sensitivity (units)	
	Before GBS procedure	One month after GBS procedure
Non-diabetic	0.55 (± 0.32)	1.30 (± 0.88)
Type 2 diabetes	0.40 (± 0.24)	1.10 (± 0.87)

a)   **Use the data in the table** to support the following conclusions.

(i)   Non-diabetic patients were at higher risk of developing diabetes following the GBS procedure.

_____

_____

_____

(ii) GBS helped many patients with type 2 diabetes but some were not helped.

_____

_____

_____

b)   Describe the effects of insulin on liver cells in non-diabetic patients.

_____

_____

_____

_____

[Model answers on page 125]

CAS
KA 2.8
Page 13

HTP
Page 112

1

Selecting
A

2

Selecting
AA

2

dKU
CA

STUDENT
MARKS   MARGIN

9 The diagram below shows stages in thrombosis within a blood vessel.

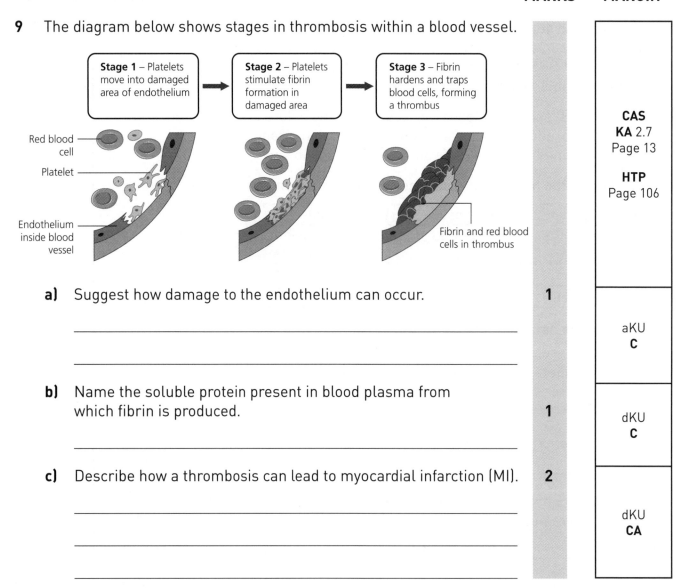

| | CAS
KA 2.7
Page 13

HTP
Page 106 |

a) Suggest how damage to the endothelium can occur.

1

aKU
C

_____

_____

b) Name the soluble protein present in blood plasma from
which fibrin is produced.

1

dKU
C

_____

c) Describe how a thrombosis can lead to myocardial infarction (MI).

2

dKU
CA

_____

_____

_____

[Model answers on page 125]

MARKS | STUDENT MARGIN

10 The diagram below shows the heart and some of its associated nerves.

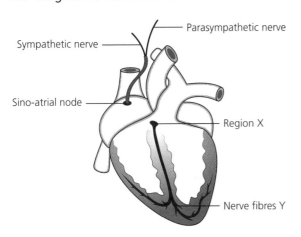

CAS
KA 2.6
Page 12

HTP
Page 97

a) (i) Name the region of the brain which regulates the sino-atrial node (SAN) through the action of the sympathetic and parasympathetic nerves shown.

1

dKU
C

(ii) The sympathetic and parasympathetic nerves act antagonistically.

Explain the meaning of this statement with reference to heart rate.

1

dKU
A

b) (i) Name region X.

1

dKU
C

(ii) Describe the role of region X and nerve fibres Y in the cardiac cycle.

2

dKU
CA

[Model answers on page 125]

STUDENT
MARKS   MARGIN

11 Describe the localisation of brain functions within the cerebrum and
    the role of the corpus callosum.

4

CAS
KA 3.1
Page 13

HTP
Page 135

dKU
CCCA

_____

_____

_____

_____

_____

_____

_____

_____

_____

_____

[Model answer on page 126]

MARKS **STUDENT MARGIN**

12 The diagram below shows parts of some cells in the central nervous system (CNS). Region Y contains synapses.

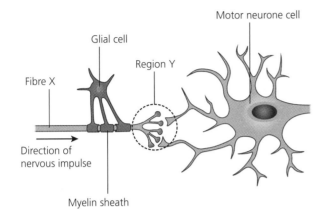

CAS
KA 3.3
Page 14

HTP
Page 149

a) **(i)** Name fibre X and give the function of the myelin sheath which has developed around it.

Fibre X _____ 1

Function of myelin sheath _____ 1

_____

_____

aKU
C

dKU
C

(ii) The specific glial cell shown in the diagram is involved in the production of the myelin sheath.

Give **one** other function of glial cells. 1

_____

_____

dKU
C

b) In region Y, nervous impulses pass across synapses.

(i) Describe how neurotransmitters are involved in the passage of nervous impulses across the synapse. 2

_____

_____

_____

dKU
CA

(ii) Name the neurotransmitters involved in reduction of pain intensity following an injury. 1

_____

dKU
C

[Model answers on page 126]

13 In an experiment into the effects of caffeine on learning, 30 25-year-old volunteers were split into three groups of ten individuals. Members of each group were given different dosages of caffeine as shown in Table 1.

Each individual was blindfolded and asked to try a finger maze as shown in the diagram below. The number of errors made during each trial was recorded and each individual completed six trials consecutively with no breaks between trials.

The results are shown in Table 2.

Table 1

Group	Caffeine dosage given (mg)
1	50
2	100
3	150

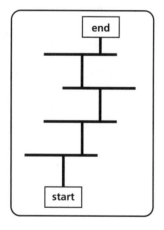

Table 2

Trial	Average number of errors per group		
	Group 1	Group 2	Group 3
1	7	6	7
2	8	6	5
3	4	3	2
4	2	2	1
5	1	0	0
6	0	0	0

a) Give a hypothesis that could be tested by this experiment.

_____

_____

1

Planning
A

Higher Human Biology

b) **(i)** Identify the dependent variable in this experiment.

1

Planning
C

_____

(ii) Identify one variable other than those already mentioned which would have to be kept constant to ensure that valid conclusions could be drawn from the results.

1

Planning
C

_____

c) Describe a suitable control for this experiment.

1

Planning
A

_____

_____

d) **(i)** On the grid below, plot line graphs to show **all** of the results of this experiment.

3

(Additional graph paper, if required, can be found on page 34.)

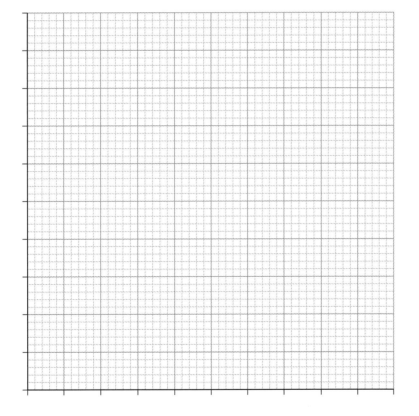

Presenting
CCC

STUDENT
MARKS   MARGIN

(ii) Give a conclusion which could be drawn from the results of this experiment.

1

Concluding
C

_____

_____

_____

(iii) Suggest an improvement to the experimental method which could increase the reliability of the results.

1

Evaluating
C

_____

_____

[Model answers on pages 126–127]

14 The bacterial species *Campylobacter*, *Salmonella* and *E. coli* 0157 each cause infections of the digestive system that result in vomiting and diarrhoea.

The chart below shows the reported number of cases of these infections in a Scottish health board area between 1991 and 1996.

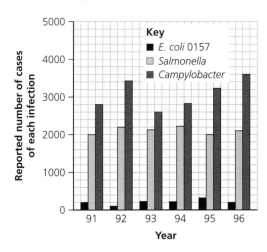

a) (i) Use values from the chart to describe the changes in the number of reported cases of *Campylobacter* between 1991 and 1996.

2

_____

_____

_____

(ii) Calculate the percentage increase in the **total** number of reported cases of these infections in 1996 compared with 1991.

1

Space for calculation

_____%

CAS
KA 3.4
Page 15

HTP
Page 171

Selecting
AC

Processing
A

STUDENT
MARKS MARGIN

b) **(i)** Suggest **one** precaution which could be taken to reduce
the number of cases of these infections.

1

_____

_____

aKU
C

(ii) Assuming that additional precautions were **not** taken,
predict the number of cases of *Campylobacter* infections
that could have been expected in 1997 in this health
board area.

1

Predicting
C

_____ cases

[Model answers on page 128]

	MARKS	STUDENT MARGIN

15 Answer **either** A or B in the space below.

Labelled diagrams may be used where appropriate.

A Describe non-specific defences against disease.

OR

	8	CAS **KA** 4.1 Page 15 **HTP** Page 171 dKU **6C2A**

B Describe the roles of T and B lymphocytes in specific immune response to disease.

	8	CAS **KA** 4.2 Page 16 **HTP** Page 175 dKU **6C2A**

[Model answers on pages 128–129]

[END OF PRACTICE PAPER A]

ADDITIONAL GRAPH PAPER FOR QUESTION 13(d) (i).

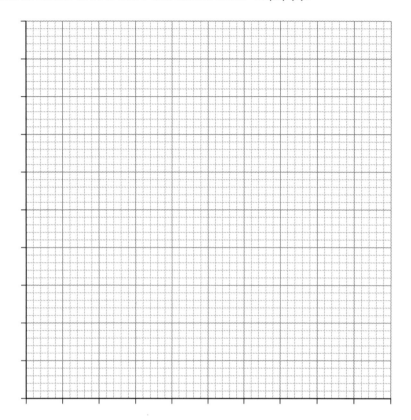

ADDITIONAL SPACE FOR ANSWERS AND ROUGH WORK

Higher Human Biology

B

Duration – 2 hours and 30 minutes

Total marks – 100

SECTION 1 – 20 marks

Attempt ALL questions.

SECTION 2 – 80 marks

Attempt ALL questions.

Question 14 contains a choice.

Write your answers clearly in the spaces provided in this paper. Additional space for answers and rough work is provided at the end of this paper. If you use this space, you must clearly identify the question number you are attempting. Any rough work must be written in this paper. You should score through your rough work when you have written your final copy.

Use **blue** or **black** ink.

Section 1

SECTION 1 – 20 MARKS

Attempt ALL questions. Answer grid available at www.hoddereducation.co.uk/updatesandextras.

STUDENT MARGIN

1   Stem cells in bone marrow give rise to:

   A   platelets only

   B   red blood cells only

   C   red blood cells and platelets

   D   red blood cells, platelets and phagocytes.

CAS
KA 1.1
Page 8

HTP
Page 1
dKU
C

2   The graph below shows changes in the number of human stem cells in a culture. The activity of the enzyme glutaminase present in the cells over an eight-day period is also shown.

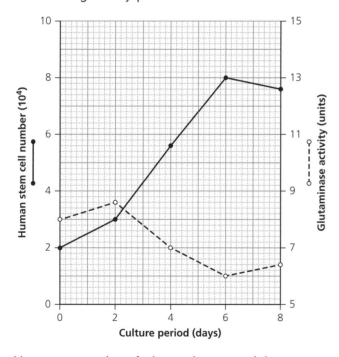

How many units of glutaminase activity were recorded when the cell number was 50% of its maximum over the eight days?

   A   6

   B   8

   C   9

   D   13

CAS
KA 1.1
Page 8

HTP
Page 1

Selecting
A

3   The graph below shows the energy changes involved in a chemical reaction.

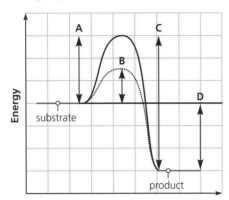

Reaction progress

Which letter indicates the activation energy of the reaction in the presence
of an enzyme?

CAS
KA 1.6
Page 10

HTP
Page 35

aKU
C

4   Which of the following gene mutations would have a frameshift effect
on the protein produced by its expression?

A   Missense

B   Nonsense

C   Deletion

D   Substitution

CAS
KA 1.4
Page 9

HTP
Page 23

dKU
C

5   Proteins may be modified before they become functional.
The list below shows changes that could modify proteins.

1   Cutting and combining polypeptide chains.
2   Adding carbohydrates to the polypeptide chain.
3   Adding phosphate to the polypeptide chain.

Which of these changes are examples of post-translational modification
of protein structure?

A   1 and 2 only

B   1 and 3 only

C   2 and 3 only

D   1, 2 and 3

CAS
KA 1.3
Page 9

HTP
Page 16

dKU
C

6   Which line in the table below correctly describes slow twitch muscle fibres?

	Main energy storage substance	Relative number of mitochondria compared to fast twitch fibres
A	Fat	Fewer
B	Fat	More
C	Glycogen	Fewer
D	Glycogen	More

CAS
KA 1.8
Page 11

HTP
Page 48

dKU
C

7   The graph below shows the concentration of lactic acid in the blood of
    an athlete and an untrained person during a 20-second period running on
    a treadmill.

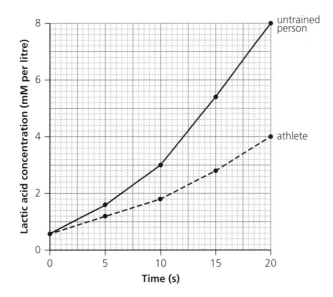

What was the average increase in lactic acid concentration per second
in the blood of the untrained person over the period?

A   0.17 mM per litre

B   0.20 mM per litre

C   0.37 mM per litre

D   0.40 mM per litre

CAS
KA 1.8
Page 11

HTP
Page 48

Selecting
A

8   Which line in the table below describes conditions related to the rhesus
    factor in which a fetus would be **most** at risk from its mother's
    immune system?

	Pregnancy	Maternal blood type	Fetal blood type
A	First	Rhesus negative	Rhesus positive
B	Second	Rhesus positive	Rhesus negative
C	Second	Rhesus negative	Rhesus positive
D	First	Rhesus positive	Rhesus negative

CAS
KA 2.4
Page 12

HTP
Page 83

dKU
C

9   Cardiac output is calculated using the formula below.

Cardiac output (l per minute) = *heart rate* (beats per minute) × *stroke volume* (cm³)

CAS
KA 2.6
Page 12

HTP
Page 97

Processing
A

The table below shows the cardiac outputs and heart rates of four individuals.

Individual	Cardiac output (l per minute)	Heart rate (beats per minute)
A	5.8	60
B	6.1	68
C	7.2	72
D	7.6	78

Which individual has the greatest stroke volume?

10 Part of an electrocardiogram (ECG) trace from an individual is shown below.

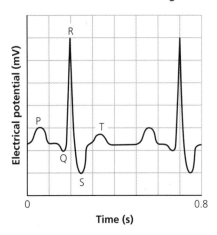

What is this individual's heart rate?

A   100 beats per minute

B   120 beats per minute

C   150 beats per minute

D   200 beats per minute

11 The ratio of high density to low density lipoproteins (HDL : LDL) in the blood is related to the level of cholesterol in the blood. Cholesterol level is related to chances of an individual developing cardiovascular disease (CVD).

Which line in the table below shows these relationships correctly?

	HDL : LDL	Level of cholesterol in the blood	Chances of developing CVD
A	High	Low	Decreased
B	High	High	Increased
C	Low	Low	Increased
D	Low	High	Decreased

CAS
KA 2.6
Page 12

HTP
Page 97

Selecting
A

CAS
KA 2.7
Page 13

HTP
Page 106

aKU
A

12 The graph below shows how the concentration of insulin in the blood of an individual was affected by changes in the concentration of glucose in their blood.

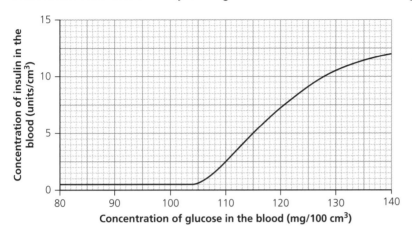

The individual has 4.8 litres of blood in their bloodstream.

What is the total mass (mg) of glucose present in the bloodstream of the individual when their blood insulin concentration is 6 units?

A 114

B 5472

C 5616

D 561 600

CAS
KA 2.8
Page 13

HTP
Page 112

Selecting
A

13 Which line in the table below identifies the cause and effect of type 1 diabetes?

	Cause	Effect
A	Lack of insulin	Failure to convert glucose to glycogen
B	Cells lack sensitivity to insulin	Failure to convert glycogen to glucose
C	Lack of insulin	Failure to convert glycogen to glucose
D	Cells lack sensitivity to insulin	Failure to convert glucose to glycogen

CAS
KA 2.8
Page 13

HTP
Page 112

dKU
C

14 The pedigree chart below shows the inheritance of Tay-Sachs disease in part of a family.

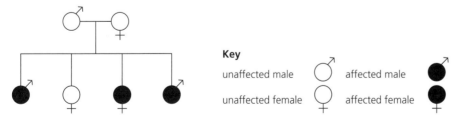

The information in the chart suggests that Tay-Sachs disease is caused by an allele that is:

A recessive and autosomal

B dominant and autosomal

C recessive and sex-linked

D dominant and sex-linked.

CAS
KA 2.4
Page 12

HTP
Page 83

aKU
A

15 The speed of transmission of an impulse along an axon fibre is increased by:

  A diffusion of neurotransmitters

  B excitatory signals

  C reverberating neural pathways

  D myelination of the fibre.

CAS
KA 3.3
Page 14
HTP
Page 149
dKU
C

16 Which line in the table below matches correctly a neurotransmitter and information related to its functions?

	Neurotransmitter	Function 1	Function 2
A	Dopamine	Reduces feeling of pain	Induces feeling of pleasure
B	Endorphins	Reduces feeling of pain	Release of sex hormones
C	Dopamine	Release of sex hormones	Reinforces behaviour in the reward pathway
D	Endorphins	Induces feeling of pleasure	Reinforces behaviour in the reward pathway

CAS
KA 3.3
Page 14

HTP
Page 149

dKU
C

17 A volunteer performed ten trials of a task involving mirror drawing.
The graph below shows the time taken to complete each trial and the number of errors made in each trial.

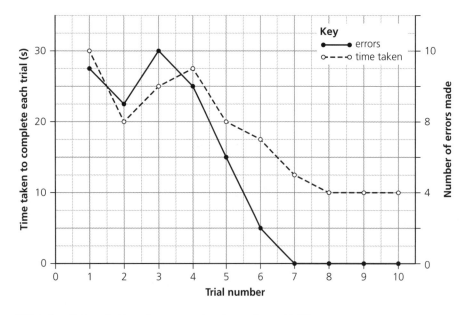

Which of the following conclusions is valid?

  A Four errors were made in Trial 8.

  B Trial 3 took 10 seconds to complete.

  C No improvement in performance was noted after Trial 7.

  D Overall performance improved between Trial 1 and Trial 4.

CAS
KA 3.4
Page 15

HTP
Page 158

Concluding
A

18 The table below shows the relative number of deaths from various causes in the population of a developing country.

Cause of death	Number (millions)
Infections and parasitic diseases	8.0
Cancers	1.8
Respiratory diseases	1.6
Circulatory diseases	5.0
Birth-related causes	2.0
Other causes	1.6

What percentage of deaths was **not** due to infections and parasitic diseases?

A   12%

B   20%

C   40%

D   60%

CAS
KA 4.3
Page 16

HTP
Page 181

Processing
A

19 Which of the following causes the production of antibodies in autoimmune disorders?

A   Viral infection

B   Harmless antigens

C   Vaccination

D   Self antigens

KA 4.2
Page 16

HTP
Page 175

dKU
C

20 Which line in the table below classifies correctly terms which describe the spread of infectious diseases?

	Regular cases in an area	Occasional cases in an area	Unusually high cases in an area	Cases occurring globally
A	Endemic	Sporadic	Epidemic	Pandemic
B	Epidemic	Sporadic	Pandemic	Epidemic
C	Endemic	Epidemic	Sporadic	Pandemic
D	Pandemic	Endemic	Epidemic	Sporadic

CAS
KA 4.3
Page 16

HTP
Page 181

dKU
C

[End of Section 1 - Answers on pages 130–131]

[Now attempt the questions in Section 2]

B

Section 2

SECTION 2 – 80 marks

Attempt ALL questions.

Question 14 contains a choice.

Write your answers clearly in the spaces provided in this paper. Additional space for answers and rough work is provided at the end of this paper. If you use this space you must clearly identify the question number you are attempting. Any rough work must be written in this space. You should score through your rough work when you have written your final copy.

Use **blue** or **black** ink.

MARKS   STUDENT MARGIN

1   The diagram below shows part of a DNA molecule and other molecules associated with it at a stage in replication.

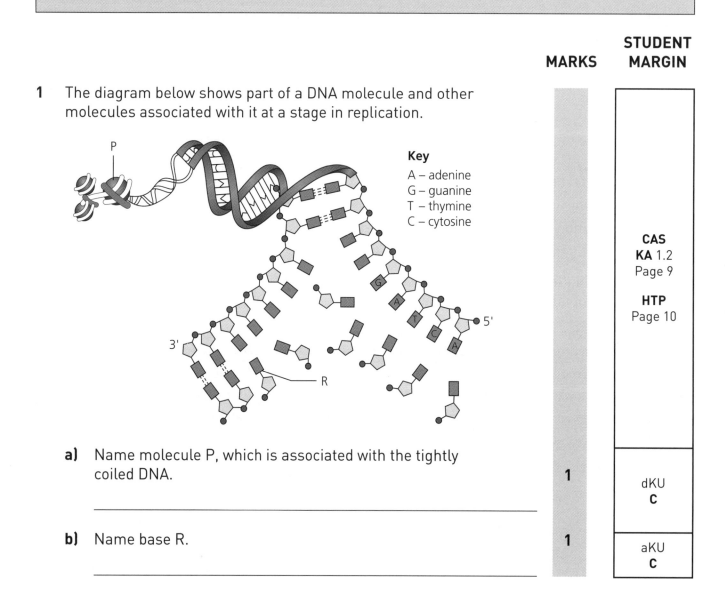

Key
A – adenine
G – guanine
T – thymine
C – cytosine

a) Name molecule P, which is associated with the tightly coiled DNA.

            1

b) Name base R.

            1

CAS
KA 1.2
Page 9

HTP
Page 10

dKU
C

aKU
C

	STUDENT
MARKS	MARGIN

c) (i) Describe how the diagram illustrates the antiparallel structure of DNA molecules.

1

aKU
C

_____

_____

(ii) The diagram shows synthesis of the leading strand of DNA.

Describe **one** difference between the replication of this strand and the other strand of the molecule.

1

dKU
A

_____

_____

[Model answers on page 132]

STUDENT
MARKS | MARGIN

2 The graph below shows how temperature is changed during three stages in one cycle of a polymerase chain reaction (PCR).

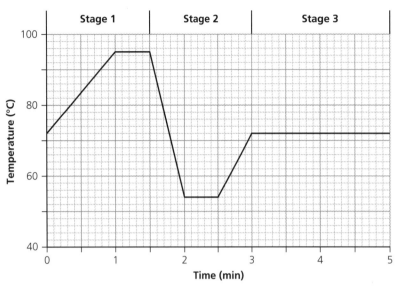

a) **(i)** State why the temperature is increased during Stage 1.

_____

_____

1

CAS
KA 1.5
Page 10

HTP
Page 29

dKU
C

(ii) Calculate the range of temperature that the PCR reaction tube experiences during one cycle of PCR.

Space for calculation

1

Selecting
C

_____°C

(iii) Short sections of DNA called primers are involved in Stage 2.

State the role of these primers during Stage 2.

_____

_____

1

dKU
C

	MARKS	STUDENT MARGIN

b) During Stage 3, high temperatures would denature most enzymes but polymerase enzymes remain active.
Explain why this is possible.

1

aKU
A

_____

_____

_____

c) Explain the role of PCR in practical applications such as forensics.

1

aKU
C

_____

_____

_____

[Model answers on page 132]

	MARKS	STUDENT MARGIN

3 Give an account of tumour production by cancer cells.

4

CAS
KA 1.1
Page 8

HTP
Page 1

dKU
CCCA

_____

_____

_____

_____

_____

_____

_____

_____

_____

_____

[Model answer on page 133]

4 Hydrogen peroxide is a toxic chemical produced in human metabolism. Catalase is an enzyme that breaks down hydrogen peroxide as shown below.

hydrogen peroxide $\xrightarrow{\text{catalase}}$ water + oxygen

An experiment was carried out to investigate how the concentration of catalase affected the rate of hydrogen peroxide breakdown.

Filter paper discs soaked in different concentrations of catalase solution were added to beakers of hydrogen peroxide solution, as shown in the diagram. The beakers were all kept at 20°C throughout the experiment.

The discs sank to the bottom of the beakers before rising back up to the surface. The time taken for each disc to rise to the surface was used as a measure of the reaction rate. The faster the disc rises, the faster the reaction rate.

The results of the investigation are shown in the table.

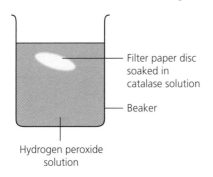

Filter paper disc soaked in catalase solution

Beaker

Hydrogen peroxide solution

Catalase concentration (%)	Average time for 10 discs to rise (s)
0.1	11.4
0.5	6.2
1.0	4.5
1.5	3.8
2.0	3.2
3.0	3.2

a) Using the information given, explain why the filter paper discs rose to the surface of the hydrogen peroxide solution.

_____

_____

1

b) (i) Give the independent variable in this experiment.

_____

1

CAS
KA 1.6
Page 10

HTP
Page 35

Planning
C

Planning
C

STUDENT
MARKS   MARGIN

(ii) Give **two** variables, not already mentioned, which should be
controlled to allow a valid conclusion to be made from the
results obtained.   2   Planning
                                                                        CA

1 _____

2 _____

c) Describe **one** feature of this experiment which helps to make
the results more reliable.   1
                                                                        Planning
                                                                        A
_____

_____

d) It was suggested that the filter paper itself reacted with the
hydrogen peroxide.

Describe how the experiment could be controlled to allow
this suggestion to be ruled out.   1   Planning
                                                                        C
_____

_____

e) On the grid below, plot a line graph to show the results of
the investigation.   2

(Additional graph paper, if required, can be found on page 65.)

Presenting
CC

MARKS **STUDENT MARGIN**

f) Give **two** conclusions which can be made from the results of this experiment.

2

1 _____

_____

_____

_____

2 _____

_____

_____

_____

Concluding
AA

[Model answers on pages 133–134]

STUDENT
MARKS MARGIN

5 The diagram below shows parts of two stages in the aerobic respiration of glucose.

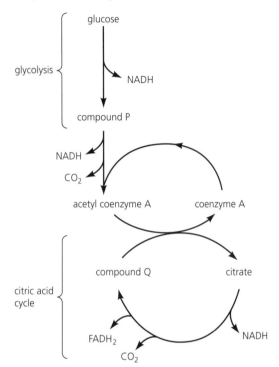

glucose

glycolysis

NADH

compound P

NADH

CO_2

acetyl coenzyme A   coenzyme A

compound Q   citrate

citric acid cycle

$FADH_2$ NADH

CO_2

CAS
KA 1.7
Page 10

HTP
Page 42

a) (i) Name compound P which is a product of glycolysis.

1

_____

dKU
C

(ii) Explain how the concentration of citrate controls the synchronisation of the rates of glycolysis and the citric acid cycle.

2

_____

_____

_____

aKU
CA

b) Name compound Q which is regenerated in the citric acid cycle and the location in cells where this metabolic pathway occurs.

2

Name _____

Location _____

dKU
CC

c) Describe the role of dehydrogenase enzymes in the citric acid cycle.

1

_____

_____

_____

dKU
A

[Model answers on page 134]

6 The graph below shows relationships between average heart rate and average arterial blood pressure in three groups of volunteers in a double-blind clinical trial. The members of the groups were given treatments as shown in the table below and the data was collected during a period of time following treatment.

Group	Treatment given
1	Drug to inhibit the action of the parasympathetic nervous system
2	Placebo
3	Drug to inhibit the action of the sympathetic nervous system

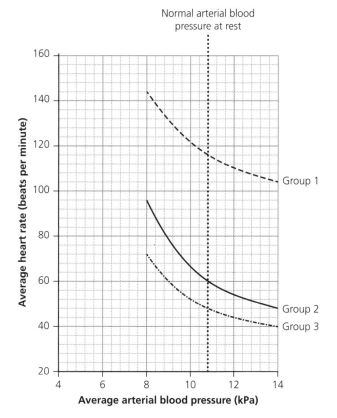

a) (i) Explain what is meant by a double-blind trial.

_____

_____

1

dKU
A

(ii) Group 3 received a placebo.

Describe what is meant by a placebo.

_____

_____

1

dKU
C

B

b) In this experiment, arterial blood pressure is measured in kPa.
Give **one** other unit which can be used to measure blood pressure.

1

CAS
KA 2.6
Page 12
HTP
Page 97
aKU
C

_____

c) Calculate the difference between the average heart rate of participants in Group 1 and those in Group 2 at normal arterial blood pressure at rest.

1

Space for calculation

_____ beats per minute

d) From the results in the graph, give **one** conclusion which could be made about the control of heart rate by the sympathetic nervous system.

1

_____

_____

e) Describe how blood pressure is involved in the creation of tissue fluid.

1

CAS
KA 2.5
Page 12

HTP
Page 91

dKU
A

_____

_____

_____

[Model answers on page 135]

7 The diagrams below represent sections through an ovary and part of a testis.

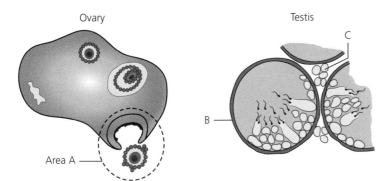

Ovary

Testis

Area A

B

C

a) Name the process which can be seen in area A and describe the role of a named hormone in its occurrence.

Name _____

Description _____

_____

2

b) Name structure B and describe its role in reproduction.

Name _____

Role _____

_____

2

CAS
KA 2.1
Page 11

HTP
Page 64

aKU
CA

c) Describe the role of the cells shown at C.

_____

_____

1

[Model answers on page 135]

STUDENT
MARKS | MARGIN

8 A study into diet and breast cancer was carried out involving 24 different countries in the world. For each country, the average percentage fat in the diet of the population was plotted against the death rates for breast cancer. The data collected are shown in the graph below.

A line of best fit was calculated and is also shown.

a) Give the data for country A.

2

CAS
KA 1.1
Page 8

HTP
Page 1

Selecting
CC

b) It was concluded that risk of breast cancer is related to the percentage of fat in the diet.

Evaluate this statement by providing one piece of evidence from the graph that supports the statement and another that does not support it.

Supports _____

Does not support _____

2

Evaluating
CA

c) The study was extended to another country, in which the average percentage of fat in the diet was 30%.

Use information from the graph to predict the expected death rate from breast cancer in this country.

_____ deaths per 100 000 people

1

Predicting
C

[Model answers on page 135]

STUDENT
MARKS   MARGIN

9   The diagram below shows a vertical section through a human brain.

Cerebral cortex of
right side of cerebrum

Corpus callosum

Cerebellum

CAS
KA 3.1
Page 13

HTP
Page 135

a) **(i)** Describe the function of the motor area in the cerebral
cortex of the right side of the cerebrum.   1

_____

_____

dKU
A

(ii) Describe the function of the cerebellum.   1

_____

_____

dKU
C

(iii) On the diagram, mark with an X an area of the brain
which contains the centres for the control of heart rate
and breathing rate.   1

aKU
C

b) Name the type of memories which are stored in the limbic system.   1

_____

_____

CAS
KA 3.2
Page 14

HTP
Page 140

dKU
C

[Model answers on page 136]

| | MARKS | STUDENT MARGIN |

10 a) Describe the importance of infant attachment.

_____

_____

b) (i) Humans have a long period of dependency on adults. State the advantage of this in human development.

_____

_____

(ii) Parents use a variety of methods to influence the behavioural development of children. Many parents set rules for their children and monitor to check that the rules are followed.

Give the general advantage of using rules and monitoring as a way of influencing development of children.

_____

_____

MARKS: 1, 1, 1

STUDENT MARGIN:

CAS
KA 3.4
Page 15

HTP
Page 158

dKU
C

aKU
C

aKU
A

[Model answers on page 136]

11 The diagram below shows part of a neural pathway which controls the action of the hand.

The arrows show the direction of the nervous impulses.

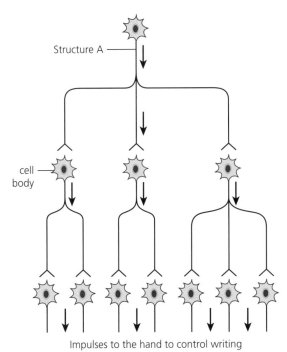

Structure A

cell
body

Impulses to the hand to control writing

a) **(i)** Name the type of neural pathway illustrated by the diagram.

1

CAS
KA 3.3
Page 14

HTP
Page 149

aKU
C

(ii) Describe how this pathway could control complex functions such as the use of the hand in writing.

2

aKU
AC

b) Name structure A.

1

aKU
C

c) Nervous impulses pass between neurons by chemical transmission at synapses.

(i) Explain why neurotransmitter chemicals must be removed from the synaptic clefts.

1

dKU
A

(ii) Describe the effect of an injection of an antagonistic drug on the neural pathway shown in the diagram above.

1

aKU
C

[Model answers on pages 136–137]

STUDENT
MARKS MARGIN

12 The diagram below represents the structure of a modified influenza virus used in vaccinations.

Surface protein

Nucleic acid

CAS
KA 4.2
Page 16

HTP
Page 175

a) **(i)** In the preparation of a vaccine from this virus, the nucleic acid is destroyed but the surface protein molecules are left intact.

Name the surface proteins and explain why they must remain intact.

Name _____

Explanation _____

_____

2

dKU
CA

(ii) Different vaccines are needed for different influenza strains. Explain why the different vaccines are needed.

_____

_____

1

aKU
C

(iii) Some vaccines have aluminium hydroxide added to enhance their activity.

Give the term used for substances such as aluminium hydroxide in the production of vaccines.

_____

1

dKU
C

STUDENT
MARKS   MARGIN

b) The graph below shows the number of cases of whooping cough reported in a developed country between 1965 and 1995 and the percentage of infants vaccinated against the disease.

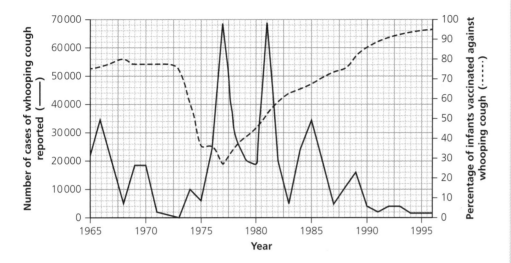

Concluding
AC

(i) Suggest **two** reasons which could explain why the percentage of infants vaccinated changed between 1972 and 1975.

2

1_____

2_____

(ii) Between 1980 and 1990, there were three peaks in the number of reported cases of whooping cough.

Use information from the graph to suggest why the number of cases of whooping cough shown by these peaks decreased over the period.

1

Concluding
A

_____

_____

(iii) Explain why the percentage of the target population vaccinated does not need to be 100% to be effective in controlling the spread of whooping cough.

1

dKU
A

_____

_____

[Model answers on page 137]

13 A healthy individual aged 25 years carried out a 6-month training programme.

Graph 1 shows the effect of a standard exercise on the individual's heart rate before and after the training programme.

Graph 2 shows the relationship between the individual's stroke volume and heart rate before and after the training programme.

Graph 1

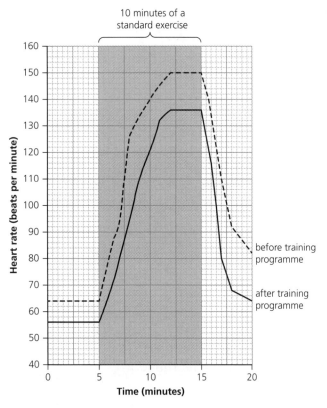

Graph 2

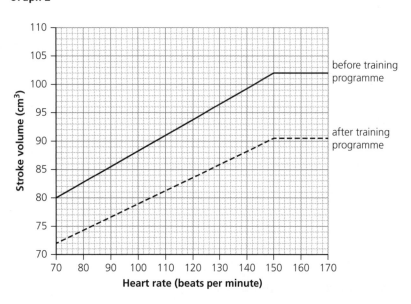

	MARKS	STUDENT MARGIN

a) Using data from **Graph 1**:

   (i) Express, as a simple whole number ratio, the individual's resting heart rate before and after the training programme.   **1**   Processing **C**

   Space for calculation

_____ : _____

Before the training programme : After the training programme

   (ii) Calculate the difference in heart rate of the individual at the end of 10 minutes of a standard exercise before and after the training programme.   **1**   Processing **C**

   Space for calculation

_____ bpm

   (iii) Calculate the number of minutes into the standard exercise at which the training programme has made the most difference to the individual's heart rate.   **1**   Selecting **A**

   Space for calculation

_____ minutes

b) Use values from **Graph 2** to describe how stroke volume is affected when heart rate changes before the training programme.   **2**   Selecting **AC**

_____

_____

_____

_____

_____

c) From **Graphs 1** and **2**:

Calculate the cardiac output of the trained athlete 5 minutes after the start of the exercise.   **1**   Processing **A**

Space for calculation

_____ cm³ per minute

[Model answers on pages 137–138]

	MARKS	STUDENT MARGIN

14 Answer **either** A or B in the space below.

Labelled diagrams may be used where appropriate.

A Describe procedures that can be used to treat infertility.

8

CAS
KA 2.3
Page 11

HTP
Page 74
6C2A

OR

B Describe the screening and testing procedures which may be carried out as part of antenatal care.

8

CAS
KA 2.4
Page 12

HTP
Page 83
6C2A

[Model answers on pages 138–139]

[END OF PRACTICE PAPER B]

ADDITIONAL GRAPH PAPER FOR QUESTION 4 (e).

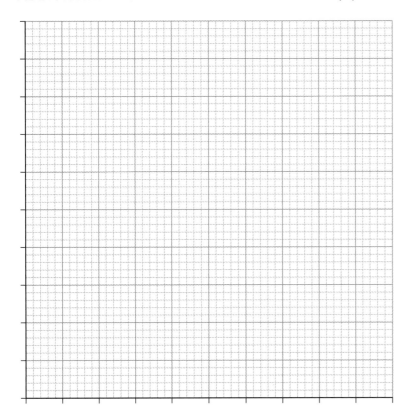

ADDITIONAL SPACE FOR ANSWERS AND ROUGH WORK

Higher Human Biology

Duration – 2 hours and 30 minutes

Total marks – 100

SECTION 1 – 20 marks

Attempt ALL questions.

SECTION 2 – 80 marks

Attempt ALL questions.

Question 14 contains a choice.

Write your answers clearly in the spaces provided in this paper. Additional space for answers and rough work is provided at the end of this paper. If you use this space, you must clearly identify the question number you are attempting. Any rough work must be written in this paper. You should score through your rough work when you have written your final copy.

Use **blue** or **black** ink.

Section 1

SECTION 1 – 20 MARKS

Attempt ALL questions. Answer grid available at www.hoddereducation.co.uk/updatesandextras.

STUDENT MARGIN

1   A DNA molecule contained 16 000 nucleotides, of which 30% contained thymine.
    How many nucleotides in this molecule would contain cytosine?

   A   1600

   B   2400

   C   3200

   D   6400

CAS
KA 1.2
Page 9

HTP
Page 10

Processing
C

2   The table below contains descriptions of DNA transcription and DNA replication which may be true or false.

   Which line in the table is fully correct?

	Description	Transcription of DNA	DNA replication
A	Occurs in the nucleus	False	True
B	Requires primers	True	False
C	Involves base pairing	False	True
D	Synthesises RNA	True	False

CAS
KA 1.3
Page 9

HTP
Page 16

dKU
C

3   The list below shows different mutations which can affect a single gene.

   1   Nonsense

   2   Missense

   3   Frameshift

   Which of these gene mutations results in the synthesis of a polypeptide which contains significantly fewer amino acids than would normally be expected?

   A   1 only

   B   1 and 2 only

   C   1 and 3 only

   D   3 only

CAS
KA 1.4
Page 9

HTP
Page 23

dKU
C

4 There are two types of human stem cell:

1 Embryonic stem cells

2 Tissue (adult) stem cells

Which row in the table describes properties of embryonic and tissue (adult) stem cells correctly?

	Properties of stem cell		
	Self-renewal	Can differentiate	Are multipotent
A	1 only	1 only	Both 1 and 2
B	Both 1 and 2	Both 1 and 2	2 only
C	1 only	Both 1 and 2	1 only
D	Both 1 and 2	1 only	Both 1 and 2

CAS
KA 1.1
Page 8

HTP
Page 1

dKU
A

5 The diagram below shows substances in a branched metabolic pathway. Substance 1 is in steady supply from the diet.

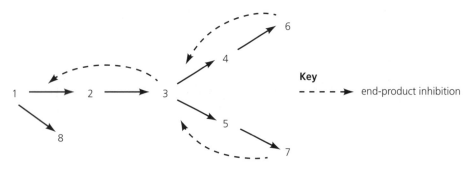

Which reaction would speed up if Substances 6 and 7 were present in high concentrations?

A $3 \rightarrow 4$

B $2 \rightarrow 3$

C $5 \rightarrow 7$

D $1 \rightarrow 8$

CAS
KA 1.6
Page 10

HTP
Page 35

aKU
C

6 Liver tissue contains an enzyme which breaks down alcohol. The graph below shows the effect of copper ions on the breakdown of alcohol by this enzyme over a 30-minute period.

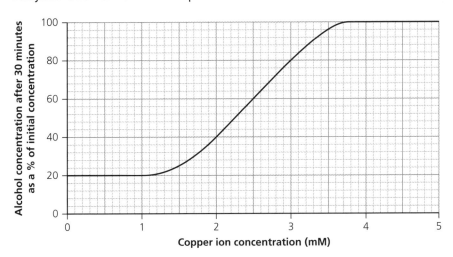

Which of the following conclusions can be drawn from the graph?

A 4.5 mM copper has no effect on enzyme activity.

B 2.5 mM copper halves the enzyme activity.

C 0.5 mM copper completely inhibits enzyme activity.

D Increasing copper from 1 mM to 3 mM increases enzyme activity.

CAS
KA 1.6
Page 10

HTP
Page 35

Concluding
A

7 In an experiment to show the effects of ATP on muscle fibre contraction, pieces of muscle measuring 50 mm were placed into 1% ATP solutions and their lengths measured after 5 minutes of immersion.

Which of the following would make the best control for this experiment?

Repeat the experiment but with pieces of muscle fibre:

A in glucose solution

B in distilled water

C in 2% ATP solution

D left out of any solution.

CAS
KA 1.7
Page 10

HTP
Page 42

Planning
C

8 The diagram below represents the days of a normal 30-day menstrual cycle.

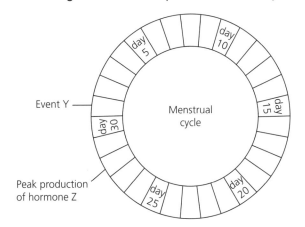

CAS
KA 2.2
Page 11

HTP
Page 68

aKU
C

Which row in the table below correctly identifies event Y and hormone Z?

	Event Y	Hormone Z
A	Ovulation	Progesterone
B	Onset of menstruation	Oestrogen
C	Ovulation	Oestrogen
D	Onset of menstruation	Progesterone

9 The following procedures can be used in the treatment of infertility:

1 Artificial insemination

2 Intracytoplasmic sperm injection

3 Pre-implantation genetic screening

Which of these procedures require *in vitro* fertilisation (IVF) as part of the fertility treatment?

A 1 and 2 only

B 2 and 3 only

C 1 and 3 only

D 3 only

CAS
KA 2.3
Page 11

HTP
Page 74

dKU
C

10 The diagram below shows a section through the heart.

At which point on the diagram would the atrioventricular node (AVN) be found?

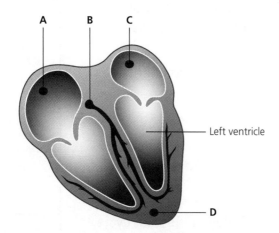

Left ventricle

CAS
KA 2.6
Page 12

HTP
Page 97

aKU
C

11 The average durations of diastole and systole in a hospital patient over a period of time were measured and are shown below.

Diastole = 0.35 seconds
Atrial systole = 0.15 seconds
Ventricular systole = 0.30 seconds

What was the average heart rate of this individual over the period of time?

A 48 beats per minute

B 70 beats per minute

C 75 beats per minute

D 80 beats per minute

CAS
KA 2.6
Page 12

HTP
Page 97

Processing
C

Higher Human Biology

12 The diagram below shows the roles of three hormones in the feedback control of sperm production.

Key

→ hormone with stimulatory effects

- - - → hormone with inhibitory effects

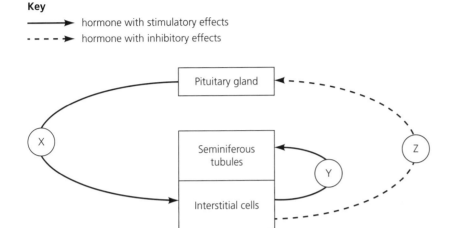

Which row in the table identifies the hormones involved at positions X, Y and Z in the diagram?

	X	Y	Z
A	ICSH	Testosterone	ICSH
B	ICSH	Testosterone	Testosterone
C	FSH	ICSH	Testosterone
D	FSH	ICSH	ICSH

13 The pedigree diagram below shows the inheritance of the metabolic disorder phenylketonuria (PKU) through three generations of a family. The allele coding for PKU is autosomal recessive.

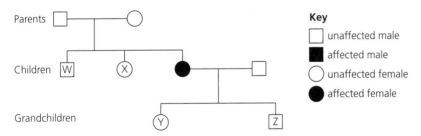

Key

☐ unaffected male

■ affected male

○ unaffected female

● affected female

Which of the individuals in the pedigree diagram **must** be heterozygous for the PKU allele?

A W, X, Y and Z

B W and X only

C Y and Z only

D X and Y only

CAS KA 2.2
Page 11

HTP
Page 68

aKU
C

CAS KA 2.4
Page 12

HTP
Page 83

aKU
A

14 The diagram below shows the stages of development of an embryo and fetus during which major or minor malformations of certain organs may occur if there is exposure to nicotine.

Key

■ major malformation
□ minor malformation

	Stage of development (weeks after fertilisation)														
	Ball of cells		Embryo (organ formation)						Fetus (organ growth and development)						
	1	2	3	4	5	6	7	8	9	10	11	12	13	14	15
brain															
ears															
limbs															
genitals															

During how many weeks after fertilisation is there risk of **only** minor malformations to the brain **and** genitals if there is exposure to nicotine?

A 5

B 6

C 13

D 15

CAS
KA 2.4
Page 12

HTP
Page 83

Selecting
A

15 The diagram below represents some neurons and the directions of impulses in a neural pathway.

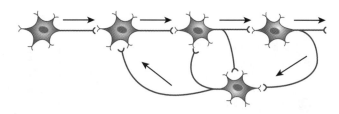

Which line in the table identifies the type of neural pathway shown and gives an example of a function in which it is involved?

	Type of neural pathway	Example of function
A	Diverging	Controlling breathing
B	Diverging	Controlling speech
C	Reverberating	Controlling breathing
D	Reverberating	Controlling speech

CAS
KA 3.3
Page 14

HTP
Page 149

aKU
C

16 The diagram below shows a vertical section of the human brain.

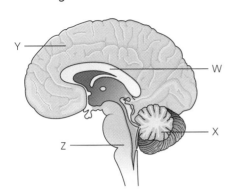

Which row in the table matches two neural functions with the areas labelled?

	Neural functions	
	Reasoned thought	Control of heart rate
A	Y	X
B	W	Z
C	W	X
D	Y	Z

17 In an investigation, the mass of myelin in brain tissue was measured in a control group without dementia and in patients with different types of dementia as shown.
Group 1 without dementia
Group 2 vascular dementia
Group 3 Alzheimer dementia
Group 4 Lewy dementia
The results are shown in the bar chart below.

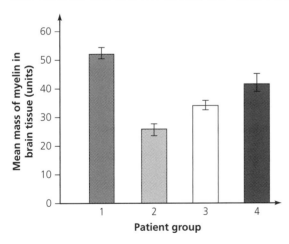

Which conclusion can be drawn from these results?

A Loss of myelin from the brain causes dementia.

B Lewy is the most severe form of dementia.

C Most myelin loss is linked with vascular dementia

D Alzheimer dementia is more severe than Lewy dementia.

C

STUDENT
MARGIN

CAS
KA 3.1
Page 13

HTP
Page 135

dKU
C

CAS
KA 3.3
Page 14

HTP
Page 149

Concluding
A

18 In a clinical trial of a new vaccine, volunteers were split into two groups: A and B.

Each group contained individuals matched on their age profiles.

Group A was given injections of the new vaccine and Group B was given injections of sugar solution.

Which of the following protocols is being described here?

A Placebo control

B Pedigree analysis

C Double-blind procedure

D Randomised treatments

CAS
KA 4.4
Page 16

HTP
Page 184

aKU
C

19 Many pathogens have evolved mechanisms which evade the specific immune system.

In which disease do the pathogens survive within phagocytes to avoid immune detection?

A Malaria

B AIDS

C Tuberculosis

D Influenza

CAS
KA 4.4
Page 16

HTP
Page 184

dKU
C

20 The table below contains information about the number of cases of influenza in a health board area over a five-year period.

Year	Influenza cases in January	Influenza cases in July
2011	580	120
2012	620	345
2013	1200	350
2014	120	145
2015	400	100

Which conclusion can be drawn from the information in the table?

A There are always more cases of influenza in January than in July.

B The number of influenza cases in January increased steadily from 2011 until 2015.

C More people died of influenza in 2013 than any other year.

D The number of cases of influenza decreased by 75% between January and July 2015.

CAS
KA 4.3
Page 16

HTP
Page 181

Concluding
C

[End of Section 1 – Answers on pages 140–141]

[Now attempt the questions in Section 2]

Section 2

SECTION 2 – 80 marks

Attempt ALL questions.

Question 14 contains a choice.

Write your answers clearly in the spaces provided in this paper. Additional space for answers and rough work is provided at the end of this paper. If you use this space you must clearly identify the question number you are attempting. Any rough work must be written in this space. You should score through your rough work when you have written your final copy.

Use **blue** or **black** ink.

	MARKS	STUDENT MARGIN

1 a) The table below shows information about cell types and cell division in the body.

Complete the table by adding the appropriate terms.

3

CAS
KA 1.1
Page 8

HTP
Page 1

dKU
CCA

Parent cell type	Type of cell division	Daughter cell type
Somatic		
Germline		Gamete

b) Body organs are formed from a variety of tissues.

Name two body tissue types.

2

dKU
CC

1 _____

2 _____

[Model answers on page 142]

MARKS **STUDENT MARGIN**

2 The diagram below shows the synthesis of a polypeptide in a cell.

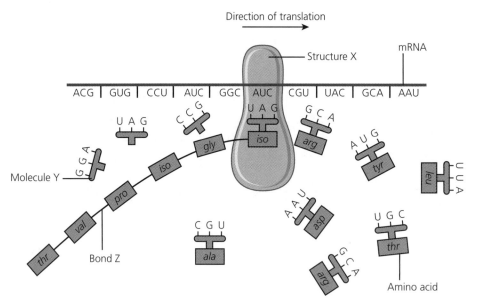

CAS
KA 1.3
Page 9

HTP
Page 16

a) Name structure X and molecule Y.

Structure X_____

Molecule Y_____

2

dKU
CC

b) In the diagram above the amino acid *iso* has just been added to the polypeptide chain.

Complete the boxes below to show the missing amino acids that will be added as the polypeptide chain is completed.

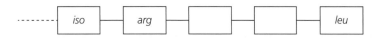

2

aKU
AC

c) Give the DNA triplet which codes for the amino acid shown as *asp*.

_____

1

aKU
C

d) Once completed, a polypeptide chain may undergo post translational modification.

Describe **one** example of a post-translational modification of a polypeptide.

_____

_____

1

dKU
C

[Model answers on page 142]

3 a) The diagram below shows parts of metabolic pathways in cellular respiration within a skeletal muscle cell.

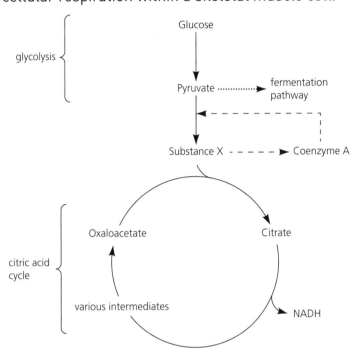

(i) Name substance X.

_____

1

(ii) The enzyme phosphofructokinase (PFK) catalyses a stage in glycolysis.

1 Describe how the activity of phosphofructokinase is regulated.

_____

_____

_____

1

2 Suggest why it is important to synchronise the rate of glycolysis with the rate of the citric acid cycle.

_____

_____

1

(iii) Describe the role of dehydrogenase enzymes in the production of NADH from the citric acid cycle.

_____

_____

_____

1

(iv) Under certain conditions, pyruvate enters a fermentation pathway as shown.

Describe the conditions under which this might occur and name the substance into which the pyruvate would be converted.

Conditions _____

Substance _____

2

CAS
KA 1.8
Page 11

HTP
Page 48

aKU
CC

MARKS

STUDENT MARGIN

b) The chart below shows the relative percentages of slow and fast twitch fibres found in the skeletal leg muscles of athletes trained for different events.

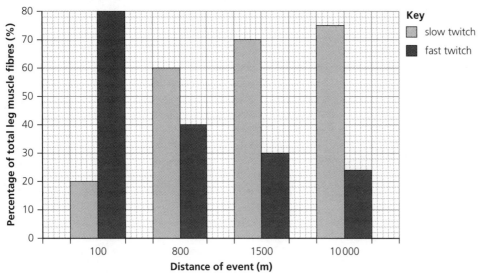

Key
- slow twitch
- fast twitch

(i) Describe the trend in the fast twitch fibre percentage data shown in the chart.

_____

_____

1

Selecting
C

(ii) Express, as a simple whole number ratio, the percentage of fast twitch muscle fibres in the leg muscles of the 100 m athlete compared to the 10 000 m athlete.

Space for calculation

1

Processing
C

_____ : _____

100 m athlete   10 000 m athlete

[Model answers on pages 142–143]

4 The diagram below shows the evolutionary relationships and origins of humans and some other species.

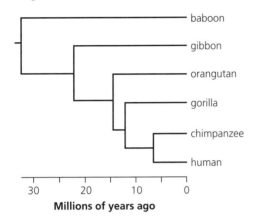

baboon

gibbon

orangutan

gorilla

chimpanzee

human

30   20   10   0

Millions of years ago

a) Describe the molecular evidence which allows diagrams such as this to be constructed.

1

_____

_____

b) Estimate how long ago the last common ancestor of humans and orangutans existed.

1

_____ million years ago

c) Explain how the analysis of individual genomes may lead to personalised medicine.

2

_____

_____

_____

CAS
KA 1.5
Page 10

HTP
page 29

aKU
A

aKU
C

dKU
CA

[Model answers on page 143]

5 The diagram below shows a cross section through a vein in an individual's leg.

- Layer P
- Central lumen
- Part of valve
- Thin layer of smooth muscle fibres

a) Name layer P, which lines the central lumen of the vein.

_____

b) Describe the role of valves and explain why they are needed in leg veins as shown.

Role _____

_____

Explanation _____

_____

c) (i) State what is meant by a deep vein thrombosis (DVT).

_____

_____

(ii) Describe the direct effects that DVT can have on the body.

_____

_____

[Model answers on page 143]

CAS
KA 2.5
Page 12

HTP
Page 91

aKU
C

dKU
CA

CAS
KA 2.7
Page 13

HTP
Page 106
dKU
C

aKU
A

6 The graph below shows changes in the concentration of glucose and insulin in the blood of a runner over a period of two hours of steady jogging.

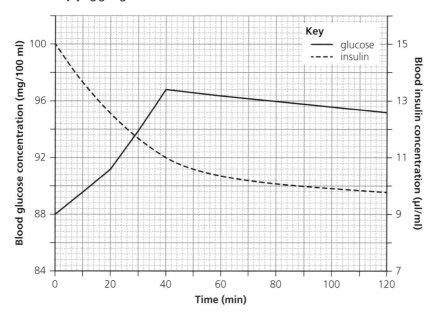

CAS
KA 2.8
Page 13

HTP
Page 112

a) (i) Give the insulin level present in the runner's blood 10 minutes after starting the jog.

_____ μl/ml

1

Selecting
C

(ii) Give the blood glucose concentration when the insulin level was 11 μl/ml.

_____ mg/100ml

1

Selecting
A

b) The adrenaline levels in the runner's blood increased throughout the two-hour period.

Explain the importance of this to the runner.

_____

_____

_____

2

aKU
CA

c) Describe how insulin is involved in type 2 diabetes.

_____

_____

_____

1

dKU
A

[Model answers on page 143]

MARKS | STUDENT MARGIN

7 The diagram below shows cells in a region of the skin which has been damaged through accidental piercing by a metal pin.

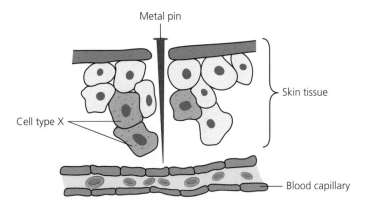

The flowchart below shows some of the events which can result from the damage of the skin.

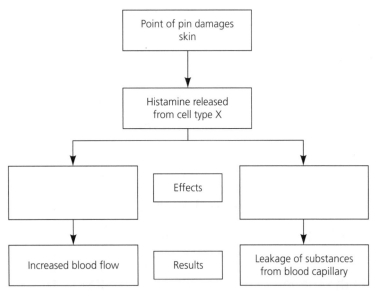

CAS
KA 4.1
Page 15

HTP
Page 171

a) Identify cell type X.

_____

1

aKU
C

b) **Complete the flow chart above** to show the effects of histamine release.

2

dKU
AC

c) Name **one** substance which leaks from blood capillaries and describe how it protects against infection.

2

Substance _____

Description _____

_____

_____

dKU
CA

[Model answers on page 144]

8 The chart below shows some processes involved in memory.

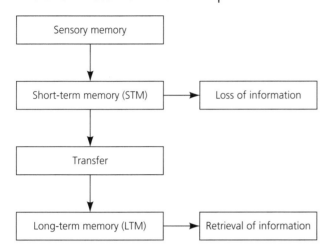

CAS
KA 3.2
Page 14

HTP
Page 140

a) Explain why loss of information from the short-term memory
can occur as shown in the chart.

1

aKU
C

_____

_____

_____

b) One method of transferring information to the long-term
memory as shown in the chart involves elaborative encoding.

(i) Give **one** other method of information transfer.

1

dKU
C

_____

(ii) Describe how elaborative encoding differs from shallow
encoding.

1

_____

dKU
A

_____

c) Suggest the effect of damage to the limbic system on the
memory of the affected individual.

1

aKU
A

_____

[Model answers on page 144]

9   Receptors on the membranes of neurons are activated by natural
    neurotransmitters and by agonistic drugs which mimic
    neurotransmitter action. Activation of these receptors produces
    an electrical response by the neuron.

    Graph 1 shows the results of an investigation into the effects of the
    concentration of the agonistic drugs morphine and buprenorphine
    on the electrical response of neurons.

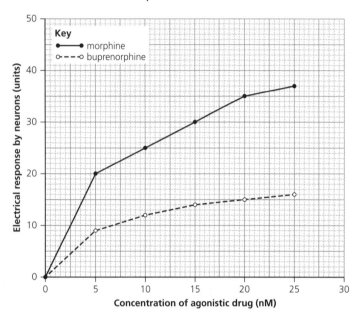

Antagonistic drugs can block the effects of neurotransmitters
and agonistic drugs.

Graph 2 shows how neurons treated with a 3 nM solution of
morphine responded to increasing concentration of an
experimental antagonistic drug.

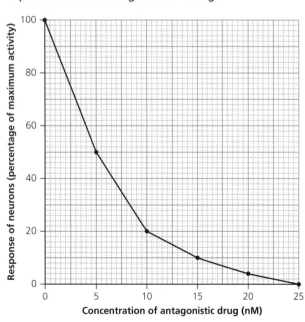

CAS
KA 3.3
Page 14

HTP
Page 149

a) Using information in **Graph 1**:

(i) Calculate the difference in response between the use of 15 nM morphine and 15 nM buprenorphine.

Space for calculation

1

Processing
A

_____ units

(ii) Calculate the percentage increase in response when the concentration of morphine was increased from 5 nM to 10 nM.

Space for calculation

1

Processing
A

_____ %

(iii) **Using values from Graph 1**, describe the effect of increasing the concentration of morphine on the electrical response by neurons.

2

_____

_____

_____

Selecting
CA

(iv) Predict the electrical response of neurons if they were exposed to 30 nM of morphine.

_____ units

1

Predicting
C

b) Using information in **Graphs 1** and **2**, calculate the electrical activity in the neurons which had been exposed to 3 nM morphine and 5 nM of the experimental antagonistic drug.

Space for calculation

1

Processing
A

_____ units

c) Using information in **Graph 2**, give the concentration of the antagonistic drug needed to reduce the neuron response by 70%.

_____ nM

1

Selecting
A

[Model answers on page 144]

C

MARKS

10 a) The diagrams below represent examples of a form of communication.

CAS
KA 3.4
Page 15

HTP
Page 158

(i) Name this form of communication.   1

_____

aKU
C

(ii) Describe **one** way in which this form of communication is important to humans.   1

_____

_____

_____

aKU
C

b) Riding a bicycle is a motor skill which has to be learned.

aKU
C

(i) Describe the effect on the nervous system of the repeated use of a motor skill such as riding a bike.   1

_____

_____

(ii) Suggest how shaping could be used by an adult teaching a child to ride a bicycle.   2

_____

_____

_____

aKU
CA

(iii) It was suggested that falls in the early stages of learning to cycle can produce a fear of bicycles and cycling.

Give the term used to describe this type of effect.   1

_____

aKU
C

[Model answers on page 145]

11 a) The diagram below shows how a cell in an individual's immune system responds to the polio virus in a vaccine.

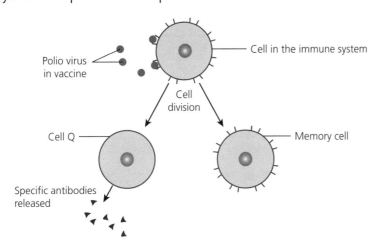

CAS
KA 4.2
Page 16

HTP
Page 175

(i) Name the substances present in vaccines that trigger an immune response.

1

dKU
C

_____

(ii) Name cell type Q.

1

aKU
C

_____

(iii) Describe the specificity of the antibodies shown in the diagram.

1

_____

_____

aKU
A

_____

b) Natural killer (NK) cells induce apoptosis in cells which have become infected with the virus.

Describe how apoptosis occurs.

1

CAS
KA 4.1
Page 15

HTP
Page 171

dKU
A

_____

_____

_____

[Model answers on page 145]

12 As part of a series of clinical trials, the systolic and diastolic blood pressures of six young adult participants were measured. Each participant was asked to drink 500 cm^3 of an energy drink and their blood pressure was measured again one hour after taking the drink.

The results are shown in the table below.

Participant	Initial blood pressure (mm Hg)		Blood pressure one hour after taking the drink (mm Hg)	
	Systolic	Diastolic	Systolic	Diastolic
1	120	75	134	82
2	127	80	145	84
3	118	70	124	72
4	134	81	143	83
5	122	73	133	77
6	129	83	137	88
Average reading	125	77	136	81

CAS
KA 2.6
Page 12

HTP
Page 97

a) Calculate the percentage increase in the diastolic pressure of participant 2 one hour after taking the energy drink.

Space for calculation

1

Processing
A

_____ %

b) (i) Give the dependent variable for this investigation.

_____

_____

1

Planning
C

(ii) Identify **one** variable, not already mentioned, which would have to be kept constant during this investigation.

_____

1

Planning
C

c) Describe an appropriate control for this investigation.

_____

_____

1

Planning
C

		MARKS	STUDENT MARGIN

d) On the grid provided, draw a bar chart to show all the average blood pressure readings shown in the table.

(Additional graph paper, if required, can be found on page 94.)

2

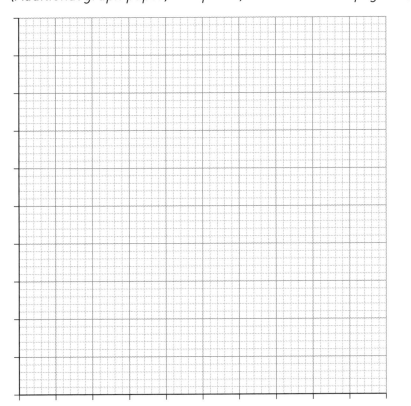

Presenting
CC

e) **(i)** Give **one** conclusion which could be drawn from the results in the table.

_____

_____

_____

1

Concluding
C

(ii) Suggest why conclusions from these results might not be valid.

_____

_____

_____

1

Evaluating
C

[Model answers on pages 145–146]

	MARKS	STUDENT MARGIN

13 Describe the general methods by which individuals and communities control infectious disease.

4

CAS
KA 4.3
Page 16

HTP
Page 181

CCCA

_____

_____

_____

_____

_____

_____

_____

_____

_____

_____

[Model answers on page 146]

	MARKS	STUDENT MARGIN

14 Answer **either A** or **B** in the space below.

Labelled diagrams may be used where appropriate.

A Describe the structure and replication of a molecule of DNA.

9

CAS
KA 1.2
Page 9

HTP
Page 10
7C2A

   OR

B Describe the mode of action of enzymes in the control of metabolic pathways.

9

CAS
KA 1.6
Page 10

HTP
Page 35

7C2A

[Model answers on pages 146–147]

[END OF PRACTICE PAPER C]

ADDITIONAL GRAPH PAPER FOR QUESTION 12 (d).

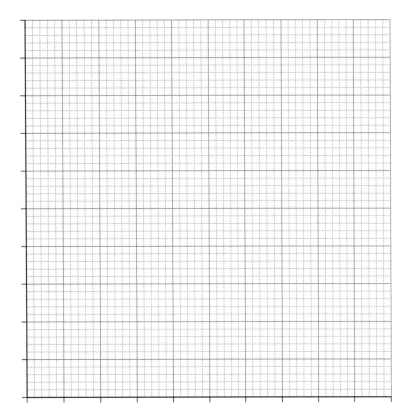

ADDITIONAL SPACE FOR ANSWERS AND ROUGH WORK

Higher Human Biology

Unit 1: Human Cells

Write your answers clearly in the spaces provided in this paper. If you require additional space for answers, use separate paper and clearly identify the question number you are attempting.

Use **blue** or **black** ink.

KA			MARKS	STUDENT MARGIN

1.1 **1** Give an account of stem cells under the following headings:

    (i) Embryonic and adult stem cells — **5**

    (ii) Stem cell research and the therapeutic use of stem cells — **3**

CAS
KA 1.1
Page 8

HTP
Page 1

dKU
6C,2A

1.2 **2** Give an account of DNA in cells under the following headings:
  (i) DNA structure
  (ii) DNA replication

5
4

CAS
KA 1.2
Page 9

HTP
Page 10

dKU
6C,3A

1.3 **3** Give an account of gene expression under the following headings:
  (i) Transcription of DNA
  (ii) Translation of mature mRNA

4
4

CAS
KA 1.3
Page 9

HTP
Page 16

dKU
6C,2A

MARKS

STUDENT MARGIN

1.4 **4** Describe the effects of named gene mutations on the amino acid sequences in proteins they code for.

7

CAS
KA 1.4
Page 9

HTP
Page 23

dKU
5C,2A

5 Give an account of the effects of mutation on health under the following headings:

(i) Effects of gene mutations on proteins synthesised

(ii) Chromosome structure mutations

3

3

CAS
KA 1.4
Page 9

HTP
Page 23

dKU
4C,2A

			MARKS	STUDENT MARGIN

1.5 **6** Give an account of DNA profiling and its applications.

6

CAS
KA 1.5
Page 10

HTP
Page 29

dKU
4C,2A

1.6 **7** Give an account of enzyme action and of the effects of competitive and non-competitive inhibition.

10

CAS
KA 1.6
Page 10

HTP
Page 35

dKU
7C,3A

1

8 Describe metabolism and the mode of action of enzymes in the control of metabolic pathways.

MARKS

9

STUDENT MARGIN

CAS
KA 1.6
Page 10

HTP
Page 35

dKU
6C,3A

1.7 **9** Give an account of respiration under the following headings:
(i) glycolysis
(ii) the citric acid cycle

3
6

CAS
KA 1.7
Page 10

HTP
Page 42

dKU
6C,3A

10 Give an account of the electron transport chain in respiration.

8

CAS
KA 1.7
Page 10

HTP
Page 42

dKU
6C,2A

| | **MARKS** | **STUDENT MARGIN** |

11 Give an account of respiration under the following headings:

    (i) The role of ATP within the cell   **4**

    (ii) The use of alternative respiratory substrates   **4**

CAS
KA 1.7
Page 10

HTP
Page 42

dKU
6C,2A

1.8 12 Give an account of skeletal muscles under the following headings:

    (i) Slow twitch muscle fibres   **3**

    (ii) Fast twitch muscle fibres   **3**

CAS
KA 1.8
Page 11

HTP
Page 48

dKU
4C,2A

STUDENT
MARKS MARGIN

13 Give an account of skeletal muscle cells under the following headings:

(i) Lactic acid metabolism — 4

(ii) Slow twitch muscle fibres — 3

(iii) Fast twitch muscle fibres — 3

CAS
KA 1.8
Page 11

HTP
Page 48

dKU
7C,3A

[Model answers on pages 148–153]

Unit 2: Physiology and Health

Write your answers clearly in the spaces provided in this paper. If you require additional space for answers, use separate paper and clearly identify the question number you are attempting.

Use **blue** or **black** ink.

KA			MARKS	STUDENT MARGIN
2.1	**14**	Give an account of the structure and function of the female reproductive system.	8	**CAS** **KA** 2.1 Page 11 **HTP** Page 64 dKU **6C,2A**
2.2	**15**	Give an account of the roles of oestrogen and progesterone in the menstrual cycle.	6	**CAS** **KA** 2.2 Page 11 **HTP** Page 68 dKU **4C,2A**

16 Write notes on negative feedback in the control of male reproduction.

9

CAS
KA 2.2
Page 11

HTP
Page 68

dKU
6C,3A

17 Give an account of the events which take place in the first half of the menstrual cycle.

9

CAS
KA 2.2
Page 11

HTP
Page 68

dKU
6C,3A

2

	MARKS	STUDENT MARGIN

18 Describe hormonal control of the menstrual cycle under the following headings:

(i) Events leading to ovulation — 6

(ii) Events following ovulation — 4

> CAS
> **KA** 2.2
> Page 11
>
> **HTP**
> Page 68
>
> dKU
> **7C,3A**

2.3 19 Give an account of the causes and treatment of female infertility. — 9

> CAS
> **KA** 2.3
> Page 11
>
> **HTP**
> Page 74
>
> dKU
> **6C,3A**

MARKS **STUDENT MARGIN**

2.4 20 Discuss the screening and testing procedures which may be carried out as part of antenatal care.

9

CAS
KA 2.4
Page 12

HTP
Page 83

dKU
6C,3A

2.5 21 Write notes on the structure and function of the arteries, veins and capillaries.

9

CAS
KA 2.5
Page 12

HTP
Page 91

dKU
6C,3A

MARKS

2.6 22 Describe the cardiac cycle under the following headings:

    (i) The conducting system of the heart   5

    (ii) Nervous control of the cardiac cycle   5

CAS
KA 2.6
Page 12

HTP
Page 97

dKU
7C,3A

		MARKS	STUDENT MARGIN

2.7 23 Describe events following the rupture of an atheroma leading to the formation of a thrombus.

6

CAS
KA 2.7
Page 13

HTP
Page 106

dKU
4C,2A

2.8 24 Give an account of the principle of negative feedback with reference to the maintenance of blood sugar levels.

9

CAS
KA 2.8
Page 13

HTP
Page 112

dKU
6C,3A

[Model answers on pages 154–158]

Unit 3: Neurobiology and Communication

Write your answers clearly in the spaces provided in this paper. If you require additional space for answers, use separate paper and clearly identify the question number you are attempting.

Use **blue** or **black** ink.

KA			MARKS	STUDENT MARGIN
3.1	**25**	Describe the structure and functions of the autonomic nervous system.	8	

CAS
KA 3.1
Page 13

HTP
Page 135

dKU
6C,2A

MARKS | STUDENT MARGIN

3.2 26 Give an account of memory under the following headings:

(i) Sensory memory

(ii) Short-term memory

(iii) Long-term memory

2
3
4

CAS
KA 3.2
Page 14

HTP
Page 140

dKU
6C,3A

STUDENT
MARKS MARGIN

3.3 27 Give an account of the structure and function of cells in the nervous system under the following headings:

(i) Neurons

(ii) Glial cells

5

3

CAS
KA 3.3
Page 14

HTP
Page 149

dKU
6C,2A

28 Give an account of the nervous system under the following headings:

(i) The role of neurotransmitters at the synapse

(ii) The structure and function of neural pathways

5

4

CAS
KA 3.3
Page 14

HTP
Page 149

dKU
6C,3A

		MARKS	STUDENT MARGIN

3.4 29 Give an account of communication between individuals under the following headings:

    (i) Non-verbal   3

    (ii) Verbal   4

CAS
KA 3.4
Page 15

HTP
Page 158

dKU
5C,2A

30 Give an account of group behaviour and social influence under the following headings:

    (i) Social facilitation and identification   3

    (ii) De-individuation and internalisation   3

CAS
KA 3.4
Page 15

HTP
Page 158

dKU
5C,1A

[Model answers on pages 159–161]

4

Unit 4: Immunology and Public Health

Write your answers clearly in the spaces provided in this paper. If you require additional space for answers, use separate paper and clearly identify the question number you are attempting.

Use **blue** or **black** ink.

	MARKS	STUDENT MARGIN

KA

4.1 31 Describe non-specific defences that the body uses to protect itself from pathogens.

9

CAS
KA 4.1
Page 15

HTP
Page 171

dKU
6C,3A

MARKS | STUDENT MARGIN

4.2 32 Write notes on specific cellular defence against infection under the following headings:

    (i) Action of B lymphocytes   4

    (ii) Action of T lymphocytes   3

CAS
KA 4.2
Page 16

HTP
Page 175

dKU
5C,2A

33 Describe how immunity is naturally acquired.   7

CAS
KA 4.2
Page 16

HTP
Page 175

dKU
5C,2A

	MARKS	STUDENT MARGIN

4.3 34 Write notes on the epidemiological terms used to describe patterns of disease occurrence and their meanings.

6

CAS
KA 4.3
Page 16

HTP
Page 181

dKU
4C,2A

35 Give an account of infectious diseases under the following headings:

(i) Methods of transmission 3

(ii) Control of disease transmission 3

(iii) Epidemiological classification of disease spread 3

CAS
KA 4.3
Page 16

HTP
Page 181

dKU
6C,3A

4.4 36 Give an account of immunisation under the following headings:
  (i) vaccination
  (ii) difficulties encountered in achieving widespread vaccination

MARKS

5
2

STUDENT
MARGIN

CAS
KA 4.4
Page 16

HTP
Page 184

dKU
5C,2A

[Model answers on pages 162–164]

[END OF EXTENDED RESPONSE QUESTION PRACTICE]

Higher Human Biology

Section 1

Question	Answer	Mark	Commentary with hints and tips
1	D	1	One strand runs from 3′ at the deoxyribose end to 5′ at the phosphate end and the complementary strand runs from 5′ to 3′.
2	D	1	The answer here is about applying the complementary base pairing rules of **A**denine pairing with **T**hymine and **G**uanine pairing with **C**ytosine. 10% = C so 10% = G. This leaves 80%, so A = 40% and T = 40%. Ratio is 10% : 40% = 1 : 4.
3	B	1	Two original DNA strands so only two cells can ever have one of these.
4	C	1	Classic translation diagram showing synthesis of polypeptide with tRNA transporting specific amino acids to the mRNA on the ribosome.
5	D	1	Remember **PCR '967'**: ● 90°C separates DNA strands ● 60°C to allow primers to attach ● 70°C optimum temperature for DNA polymerase.
6	B	1	75% of maximum of 32 = 24 (reaction rate). Draw line across from 24 until it intersects graph then take line down to X axis = 3.2.
7	C	1	Straightforward definition of feedback inhibition. Use key words from *How to Pass* to make your flashcards.
8	A	1	**ICSH** = **H**ormone that **S**timulates the **I**nterstitial **C**ells between the **S**eminiferous tubules.
9	B	1	These 'average decrease or increase' questions are often poorly done by candidates. First calculate decrease/reduction, then divide by number of years. 135 − 90 = 45 then $\frac{45}{60}$ = 0.75 million per cm^3.
10	A	1	The reaction will proceed to BQA, which will increase in concentration. Maleylacetoacetate is no longer produced so will decrease in concentration.
11	D	1	Artery endothelium is surrounded by thicker muscular wall, surrounded by elastic outer wall.
12	A	1	Plasma proteins are too large to be forced out of the capillaries and so remain in the blood plasma.
13	A	1	$75 + \left(\frac{45}{3}\right) = 75 + 15 = 90$
14	B	1	Sympathetic and parasympathetic fibres are antagonistic. Remember: ● sympathetic = 'fight or flight' ● parasympathetic = 'rest and digest'.

Question	Answer	Mark	Commentary with hints and tips
15	B	1	**PAMS** = **P**erception is **A**nalysing and **M**aking **S**ense. Visual perception is influenced by previous experience, context and expectation. Binocular disparity is related to distance perception.
16	D	1	Once again, there are many key terms and definitions required. Flashcards produced and memorised for each key area are an effective method of achieving high scores.
17	C	1	The transfer of items to the long-term memory can be brought about by **R**ehearsal, **O**rganisation and **E**laboration of meaning (**ROE**). Items can be discarded from the STM by **d**ecay or being **d**isplaced (**DD**).
18	C	1	Read across from 1 million deaths to the dotted line, then up to the solid line, then across to the infection axis.
19	B	1	**Ad**juvants **Add** to the immune response that the vaccines trigger.
20	C	1	Increase = 13 − 5 = 8 So percentage increase = $\dfrac{\text{increase}}{\text{starting value}} \times 100$ so $\dfrac{8}{5} \times 100 = 160\%$

Question			Expected answer	Mark	Commentary with hints and tips
1	a)		Differentiation	1	Changes to cells that allow them to specialise for different functions. Specialised cells express the genes characteristic of that cell type.
	b)		Tissue stem cells give rise to a more limited range of cell types than embryonic stem cells **OR** Tissue stems cells are multipotent and embryonic stem cells are pluripotent	1	Knowing the terms pluripotent and multipotent makes this question easier to answer.
	c)		**Description** (cancer cells) divide excessively to produce a mass of abnormal cells = **1** **Explanation** (cancer cells) fail to attach to each other **AND** spread through the body (to form secondary tumours) = **1**	2	Just need to know the stages of tumour and secondary tumour formation.
2	a)		Transcription	1	The name given to the copying of DNA sequences to make a primary transcript.
	b)		A triplet is a sequence of three nucleotides/bases **AND** each triplet encodes a specific amino acid	1	Triplets of bases on DNA and mRNA are called codons. Each triplet/codon codes for a specific amino acid.
	c)	(i)	**RNA** polymerase	1	Make sure that you mention which polymerase is involved – no marks for polymerase alone.
		(ii)	(Splice site mutations) can result in introns being left in the primary transcript **OR** Exons being left out of the primary transcript	1	Mutation at a point where coding and non-coding regions meet in a section of DNA. A single gene mutation at a splice site could result in an intron being left in the mature mRNA and so contributing to protein structure.
3	a)		Missense = **1** Protein/polypeptide formed is shorter/contains fewer amino acids than normal = **1**	2	Remember: ● **m**issense = **m**istake in a single amino acid ● **n**onsense = **n**o further translation, i.e. a new stop codon.
	b)	(i)	A part of a chromosome is removed **AND** becomes attached to another chromosome	1	Make these terms and definitions into flashcards and memorise.
		(ii)	Deletion **OR** duplication	1	Remember **DDT** – **D**eletion, **D**uplication and **T**ranslocation.

Question			Expected answer	Mark	Commentary with hints and tips
4	a)		Q = **1** P = **1**	2	'Before and after' shows substrate molecule P broken into products S and T. Inhibitor Q acts as a non-competitive inhibitor and attaches to a site on the enzyme other than the active site and changes the shape of the active site.
	b)		Non-competitive = **1** Inhibitor molecule binds to the enzyme molecule **AND** changes the shape of the active site = **1**	2	Enzyme inhibition by a substance that permanently alters the active site of the enzyme.
5	a)	(i)	3.0 mM per litre	1	Take care with these double Y axes graphs. Use a ruler to intersect the correct plot and then make sure that you read the value from the correct axis. In this case on the right-hand axis.
		(ii)	0.3 mM per litre	1	These 'average increase' questions are often poorly done by candidates. First calculate the increase and then divide by the number of seconds. $7 - 1 = 6$ then $\frac{6}{20} = 0.3$ mM per litre
		(iii)	1.5 mM per litre	1	Use a ruler to draw a straight line across from 5 mM per litre on the right Y axis until it intersects the lactic acid plot. Next, draw a line down until it intersects the creatine phosphate plot. Then draw a line across to the right Y axis to obtain the value of the creatine phosphate.
		(iv)	**Creatine phosphate:** When activity becomes strenuous, more ATP is required and creatine phosphate is broken down to release phosphate and energy for its synthesis = **1** **Lactic acid:** When activity becomes strenuous, oxygen becomes deficient in muscle cells and some pyruvate is converted to lactic acid = **1**	2	Creatine phosphate (CP) breaks down to release energy and phosphate, which are used to convert ADP to ATP at a fast rate, and therefore help support strenuous exercise in muscle cells. In oxygen-deficient conditions pyruvate from glycolysis is converted to lactic acid.
	b)	(i)	**Untrained individual:** Middle-distance runner has more slow twitch **AND** less fast twitch than the untrained individual **OR** Converse	1	Remember: **SS** = **S**low twitch for **S**tamina Straightforward 'describe' question, selecting information and values if necessary from the data provided.

Question			Expected answer	Mark	Commentary with hints and tips
			Elite sprinter: Middle-distance runner has less slow twitch **AND** more fast twitch than the elite sprinter **OR** Converse	1	Straightforward 'describe' question, selecting information and values if necessary from the data provided.
		(ii)	High % of fast twitch is suitable for the rapid bursts of strenuous activity needed to lift a heavy weight	1	Remember: Fast twitch for Fast and Furious, e.g. sprint and power. They contract more quickly and powerfully. **FF** = **F**ast twitch **F**atigue quickly
6	a)		Luteinising hormone/LH	1	Pituitary releases **F**SH **F**irst and **L**H **L**ast
	b)	(i)	Proliferation/thickening/further development/vascularisation of the endometrium/uterus	1	Progesterone promotes the further development and vascularisation of the endometrium, preparing it for implantation of a blastocyst, if fertilisation occurs.
		(ii)	Causes endometrium to break down/ triggers menstruation	1	The decrease in oestrogen and progesterone levels causes the endometrium to break down and triggers the start of menstruation.
	c)		Pituitary = **1** Stimulates development/maturation of a follicle **OR** stimulates production of oestrogen (by the follicle) = **1**	2	FSH initiates gamete release through the development of follicles in the ovaries and the production of oestrogen from the follicles.
7	a)	(i)	She has inherited h from her father (who is X^hY) **AND** from her mother who is a carrier/is X^HX^h/is heterozygous	1	Difficult. A mark that requires candidates to describe both the male and female. The answer should refer to the single X chromosome in males and the double XX chromosomes in females and the increased chance of males inheriting the condition.
		(ii)	X^HX^h	1	S must be heterozygous. She has received the X^h from her father and since she does not show the condition must have received an X^H from her mother.
	b)	(i)	Method to obtain embryonic cells from amniotic fluid before birth (which can be cultured) = **1** Sex chromosomes in karyotype resulting from culture of amniotic cells can be examined before birth = **1**	2	Make flashcards for all of the antenatal and postnatal screening procedures and terms and get someone to test you. A karyotype is an image of an individual's chromosomes, arranged in homologous pairs. A karyotype is used to identify anomalies in the numbers or structure of chromosomes but can also reveal the sex of the fetus.

Question			Expected answer	Mark	Commentary with hints and tips
		(ii)	100%	1	A male child will receive their single X chromosome from their mother. Since the mother has the condition she must be X^hX^h and so the male child must receive an X^h and so has the condition (X^hY).
8	a)	(i)	Some patients had mean insulin sensitivity within the range for type 2 diabetic patients following GBS	1	To answer this, you need to apply the ranges provided to obtain the upper and lower values. Then compare the non-diabetic range with the type 2 diabetes range.
		(ii)	Some patients had more sensitivity to insulin following GBS = **1** Some patients had less sensitivity to insulin following GBS = **1**	2	Again, you need to apply the ranges provided to obtain the upper and lower values. Then compare the type 2 diabetes range with the non-diabetic range to see if any improved sensitivity resulted.
	b)		In non-diabetics, insulin makes the liver cells more permeable to glucose = **1** Activates the conversion of glucose to glycogen = **1**	2	Insulin makes the liver cells more permeable to glucose and activates the conversion of glucose to glycogen, decreasing the blood glucose concentration. Both permeability and storage must be mentioned.
9	a)		Physical injury **OR** infection **OR** accumulation of low-density lipoproteins	1	If an atheroma ruptures, the damage to the endothelium causes the release of clotting factors.
	b)		Fibrinogen	1	Try to memorise the clotting process by writing the events as a flowchart.
	c)		Thrombus detaches from the site of thrombosis = **1** Thrombus becomes trapped and blocks a coronary artery = **1**	2	Thrombosis is the formation of a blood clot (thrombus) in a vessel. If a thrombus breaks loose, it forms an embolus that travels through the bloodstream until it blocks a blood vessel.
10	a)	(i)	Medulla	1	Autonomic nervous system located in the medulla.
		(ii)	Sympathetic nerve increases heart rate **AND** parasympathetic nerve decreases heart rate	1	Sympathetic nerve is the 'accelerator' – speeding it up. Parasympathetic nerve is the 'brake' – slowing it down.
	b)	(i)	AVN/atrioventricular node	1	AVN between the atria and the ventricles.
		(ii)	AVN receives impulses from the SAN = **1** AVN passes impulses down the fibres Y which stimulate contraction of the ventricle walls during ventricular systole = **1**	2	This results in the simultaneous contraction of the ventricles (ventricular systole).

A

Question			Expected answer	Mark	Commentary with hints and tips
11			1 Sensory area receives incoming impulses from sense organs. 2 Motor area originates impulses to muscles for movement. 3 Association areas process information. 4 Centres include visual, auditory, language, others (any 1) 5 Information to and from one side of the body processed by the cerebral hemisphere on the opposite side. 6 Transfer of information through the corpus callosum which connects the two hemispheres. *Any 3 from points 1–5 AND 1 mark for point 6*	4	Make sure that you know some examples of the association centres of the brain. **SS** = **S**ensory area receives impulses from **S**ense organs. **MM** = **M**otor area sends impulses to **M**uscles. Think of the corpus callosum as a bridge linking the right and left sides of the brain.
12	a)	(i)	Axon = **1** Insulates fibres **AND** speeds up transmission of impulses = **1**	2	**AA** = **A** for **A**xon, **A** for impulses **A**way from the cell body. Myelination continues from birth to adolescence.
		(ii)	Support/nutrition/fighting infection/ production of CS fluid/maintaining a homeostatic environment/removal of debris *Any 1*	1	Glial cells are the most abundant cell types in the central nervous system and have a wide variety of functions.
	b)	(i)	Vesicle fuses with membrane and releases transmitter into synaptic cleft = **1** Transmitter crosses synapse and binds to receptors in post-synaptic membrane (to pass on impulse) = **1**	2	Neurotransmitters bind with receptors. It is the type of receptor involved that determines whether a signal is excitatory or inhibitory.
		(ii)	Endorphins	1	Endorphins are released from neurons involved in pathways related to the reduction of pain intensity, euphoric feelings, appetite modulation and the release of sex hormones.
13	a)		(That increased) caffeine level in blood improves/reduces/has no effect on learning (of motor tasks)	1	When an observation is made, the suggested scientific explanation for it is called a hypothesis. A possible explanation made as a starting point for further investigation.
	b)	(i)	Average number of errors per group	1	The **d**ependent variable refers to the **d**ata (results) produced.

Question			Expected answer	Mark	Commentary with hints and tips
		(ii)	Diet up to the time of the experiment **OR** Time between taking caffeine and trial **OR** External stimuli other than the maze task **OR** Method of administering the caffeine drink **OR** Concentration of the caffeine drink **OR** Gender balance/health of the participants	1	If other variables are not controlled, differences in results could be due to them and not to the independent variable under investigation.
	c)		Repeat the experiment exactly but with another group of ten 25-year-old volunteers and no additional caffeine	1	The control should be identical to the original experiment apart from the one factor being investigated.
	d)	(i)	Axes scaled **AND** labelled correctly with units = **1** Points plotted accurately **AND** connected with straight lines = **1** Correct key **OR** labelled lines = **1**	3	Marks are given for providing scales, labelling the axes correctly and plotting the data points. Line graphs require points to be joined with straight lines using a ruler. The graph labels should be identical to the table headings and units. Choose scales that use at least half of the graph grid provided, otherwise a mark will be deducted. The values of the divisions on the scales you choose should allow you to plot all points accurately. Make sure that your scales include zero if appropriate and extend beyond the highest data points. The scales must rise in regular steps.
		(ii)	Caffeine increases the rate of learning	1	The more caffeine taken in the experiment, the fewer errors made and the faster the errors cease. It is essential to relate the conclusion to the aim of the experiment which is mentioned in the stem of the question and not simply to relate caffeine to errors.
		(iii)	Repeat the experiment with more individuals	1	To improve the reliability of an experiment and the results obtained, the experiment should be repeated. Remember **ROAR**: **r**epeat and **o**btain an **a**verage, which increases **r**eliability.

Question			Expected answer	Mark	Commentary with hints and tips
14	a)	(i)	91—92 increased from 2800 to 3400 reported cases 92—93 decreased from 3400 to 2600 reported cases 93—96 increased from 2600 to 3600 reported cases *Any 2, 1 mark each*	2	Always remember to quote key values and units.
		(ii)	18%	1	First, calculate the increase or decrease. Then, express this value as a percentage: change by dividing by the original starting value then x 100.
	b)	(i)	Good hygiene/hand washing following use of toilets **OR** Appropriate waste disposal system/ quality water supply **OR** Good hygiene/hand washing before preparation of food **OR** Appropriate storage/handling of food **OR** Treating affected individuals (with antibiotics)	1	A 'suggest' question, with lots of possible answers.
		(ii)	4000	1	Make the assumption that the latest trend of increase between 1994 and 1996 will be continued into 1997.
15	A		1 Epithelial cells/skin form a physical barrier. 2 Epithelial cells produce secretions against infection. 3 Mast cells produce histamine. 4 Histamine produces inflammation/ vasodilation/capillary permeability/ increased blood flow. 5 Phagocytes/natural killer/NK cells release cytokines which stimulate the specific immune response. 6 Cytokines lead to accumulation of phagocytes at infection sites. 7 Cytokines lead to delivery of antimicrobial proteins to infection sites. 8 Cytokines lead to delivery of clotting elements to infection sites. 9 Phagocytes recognise surface antigens on pathogens.	1 1 1 1 1 1 1 1 1	In longer ER questions, it is vital to use the language that is in the CAS – this is the key to scoring marks. Use the reference in the Student Margin to find the CAS entry and the key points list in HTP. Having a few titles for each Unit well learned is a good exam revision technique.

Question			Expected answer	Mark	Commentary with hints and tips
		10	In phagocytosis pathogens are engulfed/rendered harmless.	1	
		11	Natural killer/NK cells induce virally infected cells to undergo apoptosis/produce self-destructive enzymes.	1	
		Any 8		8	
	B	1	Lymphocytes respond specifically to antigens on foreign cells/pathogens/toxins released by pathogens.	1	
		2	T lymphocytes have specific surface proteins that allow them to distinguish between body cells and cells with foreign molecules on their surface.	1	
		3	T lymphocytes induce apoptosis.	1	
		4	T lymphocytes secrete cytokines which activate B cells and phagocytes.	1	
		5	B lymphocytes produce specific antibodies.	1	
		6	Antibodies travel in blood and lymph to infected areas.	1	
		7	Antibodies recognise antigens.	1	
		8	Antigen-antibody complexes inactivate pathogens or render them more susceptible to phagocytes.	1	
		9	Antigen-antibody complexes stimulate cell lysis.	1	
		10	Some T and B cells survive as memory cells.	1	
		11	Secondary exposure to antigens results in more rapid and greater immune response.	1	
		Any 8		8	

Practice Paper B

Section 1

Question	Answer	Mark	Commentary with hints and tips
1	D	1	Tissue (adult) stem cells in bone marrow differentiate into red blood cells, platelets and the various forms of phagocytes and lymphocytes.
2	B	1	Max = 8 so 50% = 4. Use your ruler to draw a line along from the 4 on the left axis until it intersects the stem cell line, then draw a line down until it intersects the glutaminase line. Finally, draw a line over to the right axis to obtain the answer.
3	B	1	Remember: enzymes lower the activation energy needed to start a metabolic reaction.
4	C	1	Frameshift mutation affects the number of bases in the code – only deletion and insertion can do this.
5	D	1	A variety of proteins can be expressed from the same gene due to alternative RNA splicing and the various types of post-translational modification that can occur.
6	B	1	**SSMM** = **S**low twitch for **S**tamina events, **M**itochondria and **M**yoglobin. **FF** = **F**ast twitch for **F**ast events. Anaerobic and only involves glycolysis.
7	C	1	These 'average increase' questions are often poorly done by candidates. First calculate the increase then divide by the time period, in this case 20 minutes. $8.0 - 0.6 = 7.4$ then $\dfrac{7.4}{20} = 0.37$ mM per litre
8	C	1	This condition arises when the mother is rhesus negative and the fetus is rhesus positive. Red blood cells from the fetus cross the placenta at birth and sensitise her immune system. The mother can then produce antibodies which might damage a future rhesus positive baby.
9	C	1	This involves you rearranging the formula: $SV = \dfrac{CO}{HR}$
10	B	1	From this ECG, one complete trace = 0.5 s Therefore, heartbeats in 1 minute = $60 \times 0.5 = 120$
11	A	1	High-density lipoprotein (HDL) transports excess cholesterol from the body cells to the liver for elimination. Low-density lipoprotein (LDL) transports cholesterol to body cells.

Question	Answer	Mark	Commentary with hints and tips
12	C	1	$6\,units = \dfrac{117\,mg}{100\,cm^3}$ First take care that you are familiar with the scales on each axis. A concentration of 6 units of insulin/cm^3 is present when the concentration of glucose is 117 mg for every 100 cm^3. So in 4.8 litres there are: $\dfrac{4800}{100} \times 117 = 5616$
13	A	1	A person with type 1 diabetes is unable to produce insulin and is treated with regular injections of insulin. Individuals with type 2 diabetes produce insulin but their cells are less sensitive to it. This is linked to a decrease in the number of insulin receptors on the liver cells.
14	A	1	Evidence indicating recessive because neither parent is showing the condition and autosomal because if it had been sex-linked the male parent would have to show the condition for any daughters to have the condition.
15	D	1	Myelination continues from birth to adolescence.
16	B	1	Try making up flashcards with the name of the neurotransmitter on one side and the functions on the reverse.
17	D	1	Just requires careful reading of each statement to see if it applies to the data provided.
18	D	1	$\dfrac{Number\ required}{Total} \times 100$ So, add up number of deaths not caused by infection (12) then divide by total (20) then multiply by 100. $\dfrac{12}{20} \times 100 = 60\%$
19	D	1	An immune response by T lymphocytes to self antigens present in the body.
20	A	1	Flashcard terms and definitions required for this. Use the key words in *How to Pass* to make up packs for each key area then have someone test you.

Section 2

Question			Expected answer	Mark	Commentary with hints and tips
1	a)		(Associated) Protein **OR** histone	1	The histone/protein package the DNA.
	b)		Thymine	1	The answer here is about applying the complementary base pairing rules of **A**denine pairing with **T**hymine and **G**uanine pairing with **C**ytosine.
	c)	(i)	The 3′ (deoxyribose) end of one strand is bonded/joined to the 5′ (phosphate) end of its complementary strand	1	Parallel strands in DNA but running in opposite directions. Must mention the 3′ and 5′ shown in the diagram.
		(ii)	The lead strand is replicated continuously **AND** the lagging strand/other strand is replicated/built up in sections/fragments	1	A primer joins the end of the 3′–5′ leading template strand and DNA polymerase adds free DNA nucleotides to synthesise a complementary strand continuously. On the lagging strand, primers are added one by one into the replication fork as it widens and DNA nucleotides are added to form fragments. These fragments are then joined by DNA ligase to form a complete complementary strand.
2	a)	(i)	To separate the (DNA) strands/ break the hydrogen bonds between strands/denature the DNA	1	Remember **PCR '967'**: ● 90°C separates DNA strands ● 60°C to allow primers to attach ● 70°C optimum temperature for DNA polymerase.
		(ii)	41°C	1	Find the upper and lower value then subtract to find the range: 95 – 54 = 41
		(iii)	They bind/anneal/join to (the ends of the) target/complementary sequences (of DNA being copied)	1	Primers are short pieces of single-stranded DNA that are complementary to the target sequence. The DNA polymerase begins synthesising new DNA from the end of the primer.
	b)		Enzymes used in this procedure are heat tolerant/from hot spring bacteria/extremophile bacteria	1	*T. aquaticus* is a bacterium that lives in hot springs and hydrothermal vents, and the enzyme **Taq polymerase** can withstand the protein-denaturing high temperatures required during PCR.
	c)		Amplifies/makes many copies of DNA	1	PCR is now commonly used as part of a wide variety of applications, including genotyping, cloning, mutation detection, sequencing, forensics and paternity testing. Remember though, PCR only amplifies the DNA to give a big enough sample to work with.

Question			Expected answer	Mark	Commentary with hints and tips
3			1 Cancer cells have uncontrolled cell division/divide excessively. 2 Do not respond to regulatory signals. 3 Produce a mass of abnormal cells/which is a tumour. 4 May fail to attach to each other. 5 (If they fail to attach to each other) they can spread through the body. 6 This can lead to secondary tumours. *Any 4*	4	You could write this out as a flow chart.
4	a)		Oxygen is produced (becoming trapped in the filter paper, causing it to float)	1	Need to make the link between the information provided regarding oxygen gas/bubble release and how this could cause the paper discs to rise.
	b)	(i)	Catalase concentration	1	**In**dependent variables are being **In**vestigated. **D**ependent variables give the **D**ata that form the results.
		(ii)	Size/surface area/diameter/mass (weight OK)/thickness/type of filter paper/disc **OR** Concentration of hydrogen peroxide **OR** Height/depth/volume of hydrogen peroxide **OR** Height/depth/volume/size/shape/dimensions of beaker **OR** Soaking time **OR** Temperature of the solution **OR** pH of the solution *Any 2, 1 mark each*	2	Controlled variables should be kept constant. Good idea to look for mention of liquids or solutions in any investigation and then think **VC = Volume and Concentration**. Then, if enzymes are involved check to see if temperature and pH have been controlled. 'ET phone home' = **E**nzymes, **T**emperature and **pH**.
	c)		Ten discs were used at each concentration **OR** The experiment was repeated at each concentration **OR** Average time was taken for each concentration	1	**ROAR = R**epeat, **O**btain an **A**verage, **R**eliable. In this instance, we see that a table with average time has been included and so this means that the experiment had been replicated to improve reliability.

Question			Expected answer	Mark	Commentary with hints and tips
	d)		Use discs soaked in water (added to hydrogen peroxide) **OR** Use discs containing no catalase (added to hydrogen peroxide)	1	The control should be identical to the original experiment apart from the one factor being investigated. If you are asked to describe a suitable control, make sure that you describe it in full. A control experiment allows a comparison to be made and allows you to relate the dependent variable to the independent one.
	e)		Correct scales, labels and units on axes (average time(s) is acceptable) = **1** Points correctly plotted and line drawn = **1**	2	Marks are given for providing scales, labelling the axes correctly and plotting the data points. Line graphs require points to be joined with straight lines using a ruler. The graph labels should be identical to the table headings and units. Choose scales that use at least half of the graph grid provided, otherwise a mark will be deducted. The values of the divisions on the scales you choose should allow you to plot all points accurately. Make sure that your scales include zero if appropriate and extend beyond the highest data points. The scales must rise in regular steps.
	f)		1 As (catalase) concentration increases reaction rate/rate of hydrogen peroxide breakdown increases = **1** 2 At higher concentrations/above 1% the reaction rate levels off = **1**	2	When concluding, you must provide a reference to the experimental aim, which is likely to be stated in the stem of the question. This conclusion requires you to describe both clear trends shown.
5	a)	(i)	Pyruvate	1	During glycolysis, glucose is broken down to pyruvate in the absence of oxygen.
		(ii)	High citrate levels/concentrations = **1** Inhibit phosphofructokinase/PFK = **1**	2	PFK is the key regulatory enzyme for glycolysis and when ATP and citrate levels are high in the cell, the cell no longer needs metabolic energy production to occur and PFK's activity is inhibited.
	b)		Oxaloacetate = **1** Matrix of mitochondria = **1**	2	Oxaloacetate is regenerated by enzyme-mediated reactions in the citric acid cycle.
	c)		Removes hydrogen ions from/electrons from/oxidises substrate **OR** Causes reduction of NAD/FAD/hydrogen acceptor **OR** Changes NAD to NADH OR FAD to FADH2	1	Dehydrogenases remove hydrogen ions and electrons from intermediates in the citric acid cycle. Remember to use the term 'hydrogen ions'.

Question			Expected answer	Mark	Commentary with hints and tips
6	a)	(i)	Method in which neither trial participant nor experimenter knows the treatment given	1	The purpose of this kind of study is to eliminate the power of suggestion or bias.
		(ii)	(Participants are given) a treatment which does not contain the drug (under trial)	1	Researchers use placebos during studies to help them understand what effect a new drug or some other treatment might have on a particular condition. They then compare the effects of the drug and the placebo on the people in the study.
	b)		mmHg	1	The mmHg is millimetres of mercury — the units used to measure blood pressure.
	c)		56 beats per minute (± 1)	1	Read up from the normal arterial pressure at 10.8 kPa then find where the line for Group 1 cuts = 60 bpm and where the line for Group 1 cuts = 116 bpm; then subtract the values.
	d)		Sympathetic keeps heart rate up/higher/increases heart rate (compared with control)	1	Group 1 results show what happens in the absence of the parasympathetic system and so shows the sympathetic system effects clearly.
	e)		Pressure filtration/high pressure forces plasma out of capillaries and into tissue fluid	1	Capillaries are leaky so pressure within them causes squeezing out of fluid.
7	a)		Ovulation = **1** High level of LH triggers the release of a (mature) ovum (from an ovary/ into an oviduct) = **1**	2	This is the event which marks the end of the follicular phase and the start of the luteal phase of the menstrual cycle.
	b)		Seminiferous tubule = **1** Sperm production = **1**	2	Testes are made up of coiled tubules which show up as circular shapes in the diagram.
	c)		Produce/release testosterone	1	Remember this by its 'T' sound - in**T**ers**T**i**T**ial cells produce **T**es**T**os**T**erone.
8	a)		Has a diet with 35% fat on average = **1** A death rate from breast cancer of 20 per 100 000 = **1**	2	This simply requires you to take the information/values straight from the X and Y axes.
	b)		As the average percentage of fat in the diet increases, the death rate from breast cancer increases = **1** Similar death rates at different average % fat in diet = **1**	2	First statement supporting the conclusion is perhaps more obvious. Noticing the different death rates despite the same percentage of fat in the diet is more challenging.
	c)		15	1	The most obvious prediction is best obtained from the line of best fit so read up from 30% to the best fit line then across to the X axis scale.

Question			Expected answer	Mark	Commentary with hints and tips
9	a)	(i)	Controls/sends impulses to the skeletal muscles/effectors on the left side of the body	1	**MM** = **M**otor area sends impulses to **M**uscles. However, notice the reference in the stem of the question to the right side of the brain, which requires the answer to include the impulses being sent to the left side of the body.
		(ii)	Contains balance and muscular coordination	1	Make sure you don't mix up cerebrum and cerebellum.
		(iii)	Mark in region to left of cerebellum	1	The medulla is the lowest part of the brain and contains centres that control aspects of the body's involuntary autonomic responses.
	b)		Emotional/spatial memories	1	Different types of memories are stored in different areas of the brain.
10	a)		Lays the foundation for future stable relationships **OR** Allows a bond to form between mother and baby	1	Development of successful relationships starts as infants bond with their carers.
	b)	(i)	Provides time for socialisation/learning to occur	1	Humans live in complex social groups and have large brains capable of high levels of learning.
		(ii)	(Generally results in) greater social competence (than permissive control)	1	Authoritative control – parent supports, sets rules and monitors. Permissive control – parent supports, but sets few rules and relies on trust.
11	a)	(i)	Diverging/divergent	1	In diverging neural pathways, impulses from one neuron are passed to several others.
		(ii)	Impulses go to many/a number of effectors/muscles/fingers = **1** This allows fine motor control **OR** This allows coordination of the muscles/movements/fingers = **1**	2	Allows several muscles to be activated/stimulated/contracted at once and brings about the coordinated fine motor movement of the hand needed for writing.
	b)		Axon	1	**AA** = **A**xons conduct impulses **A**way from cell bodies.
	c)	(i)	To maintain sensitivity/prevent continuous stimulation/allow system to respond to new signals	1	If the neurotransmitter was left in the synaptic cleft there would be continuous stimulation of the post-synaptic membrane and the system would not be able to respond to new signals, making precise control impossible.

Question			Expected answer	Mark	Commentary with hints and tips
		(ii)	Inhibit transmission of nerve impulse **OR** Bind to receptors in the synapses	1	Antagonistic drugs block the action of natural neurotransmitters and so prevent nerve impulses passing synapses.
12	a)	(i)	Antigens = **1** To allow recognition by the immune system/lymphocytes **OR** So antibodies/memory cells can be produced = **1**	2	Surface protein is an antigen. Antigen – molecule that can produce an immune response in the body.
		(ii)	Different strains of flu/the viruses have different antigens/surface proteins/antigenic markers/show antigenic variation	1	Mutations can result in different surface proteins.
		(iii)	Adjuvants	1	**Ad**juvants **Add** to the immune response that the vaccines trigger.
	b)	(i)	1 Whooping cough cases were very low prior to 1973 **OR** disease no longer seen as a threat = **1** 2 Less promotion of vaccine **OR** negative media coverage of vaccines **OR** worry about safety of vaccine **OR** lack of vaccine/access to vaccines = **1**	2	In these questions you need to spot trends or values that may then allow you to apply your knowledge or suggest an explanation to account for the data.
		(ii)	The percentage of infants vaccinated has increased	1	Although there were three peaks, the overall trend was down and this correlates with the increase in the percentage of infants vaccinated.
		(iii)	Herd immunity threshold is lower than 100% **OR** description **OR** many vaccinated individuals protect those unvaccinated **OR** herd immunity protects individuals who have not been vaccinated	1	Herd immunity occurs when a large percentage of a population is immunised, making it harder for infections to spread.
13	a)	(i)	8:7	1	First you need to obtain the values for the ratio from the data provided in the graph. Take care that you present the ratio values in the order they are stated in the question. Then simplify them, first by dividing the larger number by the smaller one then dividing the smaller one by itself. However, if this does not give a whole number then you need to find another number that will divide into both of them; 64:56 simplifies to 8:7.
		(ii)	14	1	From Graph 1 150 – 136 = 14
		(iii)	3	1	Needs careful measurement.

Question			Expected answer	Mark	Commentary with hints and tips
	b)		Between 70 and 150 bpm stroke volume increased from 80 cm³ to 102 cm³ = **1** From 150 to 170 bpm stroke volume remains steady/constant at 102 cm³ = **1**	2	When you are asked to describe a trend, it is essential that you quote the values of the appropriate points and use the exact labels given on the axes in your answer. You must use the correct units in your description.
	c)		10 080 cm³	1	Cardiac output = Heart rate × Stroke volume. From Graph 1 – Heart rate of individual 5 minutes after the start of exercise period after the training period = 120. From Graph 2 – a heart rate of 120 gives a stroke volume of 84. So CO = 120 × 84 = 10 080
14	A	1	Ovulation can be stimulated by drugs.	1	In longer ER questions, it is vital to use the language that is in the CAS – this is the key to scoring marks. Use the reference in the student margin to find the CAS entry and the key points list in HTP. Having a few titles for each unit well learned is a good exam revision technique.
		2	These prevent the negative feedback of oestrogen on FSH production.	1	
		3	Other drugs/hormones (not FSH/LH) can be given which mimic the action of FSH/LH.	1	
		4	These cause super ovulation/the production of a number of ova/eggs.	1	
		5	*In vitro* fertilisation/IVF programmes	1	
		6	Ova are removed (surgically) from the ovaries.	1	
		7	Ova are mixed with sperm/fertilisation occurs outside the body.	1	
		8	Fertilised eggs divide to form a ball of cells/at least 8 cells form/form a blastocyst.	1	
		9	Transferred into the uterus (for implantation).	1	
		10	Artificial insemination can be used when the man has a low sperm count.	1	
		11	If the man is sterile a donor can supply sperm. Several samples can be collected from a man with a low sperm count.	1	
		12	Intracytoplasmic sperm injection/ICSI can be used if sperm are defective/low in number.	1	

Question			Expected answer	Mark	Commentary with hints and tips
		13	The head of the sperm is injected directly into the egg.	1	
		Any 8		8	
	B	1	Mother's blood pressure/blood type/blood tests/urine tests/ general health check.	1	
		2	Ultrasound (imaging/scan).	1	
		3	Dating scan/scan at 8–14 weeks is used to determine stage of pregnancy/due date.	1	
		4	Anomaly scan/scan at 18–20 weeks for serious physical problems.	1	
		5	Biochemical/chemical tests detect (physiological) changes of pregnancy.	1	
		6	Marker chemicals/named chemical can indicate medical conditions/can give a false positive result.	1	
		7	Diagnostic/further testing can follow from routine testing/ named test.	1	
		8	Amniocentesis/cells from amniotic fluid used to produce karyotype/to test for Down syndrome/chromosome abnormalities.	1	
		9	Chorionic villus sampling/CVS – cells from placenta/chorion used to produce karyotype/to test for Down syndrome/chromosome abnormalities.	1	
		10	CVS carried out earlier in pregnancy than amniocentesis.	1	
		11	Allows immediate karyotyping.	1	
		12	CVS has higher risk of miscarriage.	1	
		13	Rhesus antibody testing described (for sensitisation of Rh– mother by Rh+ antigens).	1	
		Any 8		8	

Practice Paper C

Section 1

Question	Answer	Mark	Commentary with hints and tips
1	C	1	Use the base pair rules to find out that the percentage of cytosine in the molecule is 20%. Then find 20% of 16000 = 3200.
2	D	1	Transcription and replication are similar because they both occur in the nucleus of human cells and they both rely on base pairing. However, they progress in different ways and have different functions.
3	A	1	Nonsense mutation results in an early stop to the genetic information so fewer amino acids in the polypeptide.
4	B	1	All stem cells self renew and differentiate. Embryonic stem cells are pluripotent but adult stem cells are only multipotent.
5	D	1	The end-product inhibitions would reduce the activity of enzymes working on substance 3, which would then build up inhibiting the conversion of 1 into 2 and so increase the production of 8 from 1.
6	B	1	Tricky! With 0 copper 20% of alcohol remains after 30 minutes, and at high copper concentrations 100% of the alcohol remains. At 2.5 mM 60% of the alcohol remains – that's halfway between 20% and 100%.
7	B	1	A control aims to ensure that the independent variable caused the dependent variable, so repeating the experiment exactly but leaving out the independent variable is an effective control.
8	D	1	Progesterone peaks near to the end of the cycle on day 30 and triggers the onset of menstruation.
9	B	1	To achieve 2, an ovum has to be manipulated and for 3, an embryo of a few cells has to have a cell removed. Both of these requirements mean removal of an ovum and IVF.
10	B	1	The AV node is found between the atria and the ventricles so quite easy to locate.
11	C	1	Add up all the times to find the duration of a cardiac cycle = 0.8 s, then divide 60 s by 0.8 to find the number of beats which could occur in that time = 75 beats per minute.
12	B	1	The point here is to remember that testosterone stimulates sperm production in the tubules, but when it is in high concentration it negatively feeds back to the pituitary gland so switching off its own production.
13	C	1	Although W and X **could** be heterozygous, it is not certain because they may have inherited a recessive allele from each of their parents. Y and Z **must** be heterozygous because they **must** have inherited a recessive from their mother.
14	B	1	The genitals are at risk of major malformation up to the end of week 9 so both genitals **and** brain are at risk from minor malformation for the remaining time, which is 6 weeks.
15	C	1	Reverberation occurs when the pathway loops back on itself repeating the same impulses time and again – this results in a continuously repeated action such as breathing.

Question	Answer	Mark	Commentary with hints and tips
16	D	1	Reasoned thought in the cerebrum and control of heart rate in the medulla.
17	C	1	Only C can be concluded – the others may be correct but cannot be seen from the graph alone.
18	A	1	Placebo is the technique of giving a treatment that does not contain the active ingredient as a control in a clinical trial.
19	C	1	TB bacteria can shelter within a host cell so that their antigens are not visible to lymphocytes.
20	D	1	Only option D is true and can actually be concluded from the information available. Option C is probably true but cannot be confirmed since other years are not included in the table.

Section 2

Question			Expected answer	Mark	Commentary with hints and tips
1	a)		Mitosis = **1** Somatic = **1** Meiosis = **1**	3	Somatic cells are body cells that can undergo mitosis to produce more somatic cells. Germline cells are only found in testes and ovaries and can undergo either mitosis or meiosis but only meiosis gives gametes.
	b)		Nervous Connective Muscle Epithelium *Any 2, 1 mark each*	2	There are other types of tissue but these are the ones mentioned in the CAS so you are better to stick with them.
2	a)		X ribosome = **1** Y tRNA = **1**	2	Ribosomes are the sites of polypeptide synthesis in cells and tRNA molecules carry specific amino acids to them.
	b)		*tyr – ala* *1 mark each*	2	Use the codons and anticodons to work this one out – don't just assume it will be the nearest amino acids.
	c)		AAT	1	Need to work back through the anticodon shown through the codon which would be complementary then back to the DNA triplet.
	d)		Cutting and combining polypeptides Adding carbohydrate Adding phosphate *Any 1 = 1*	1	There are many more but these are the three given in the CAS – safest to use one of them.
3	a)	(i)	Acetyl group	1	Removal of carbon dioxide from pyruvate results in an acetyl group.
		(ii)	**1** It is inhibited by ATP/citrate/citric acid.	1	This is an example of feedback inhibition – substances involved in the citric acid cycle can inhibit glycolysis.
			2 This ensures ATP is made when needed.	1	This conserves cell resources and targets them to the most vital functions.
		(iii)	Remove hydrogen ions and electrons from substrates/intermediates **AND** transfer them to NAD	1	Need to emphasise both aspects of the dehydrogenase activity.
		(iv)	Shortage of oxygen/high levels of exercise = **1** lactic acid/lactate = **1**	2	When muscles are exercising at a high level, oxygen becomes in short supply and fermentation converts pyruvate to lactic acid/lactate.
	b)	(i)	As the distance of the event increases, the percentage of fast twitch muscle fibres decreases	1	This straightforward trend does not need values to be given.

Question			Expected answer	Mark	Commentary with hints and tips
		(ii)	10 : 3	1	Read values from the chart = 80 and 24 then look for the lowest common factor = 8 and divide each chart value by this number.
4	a)		Differences between DNA sequences **OR** Amino acid sequences in protein (between the different species mentioned)	1	The more differences in their sequence data, the longer ago the common ancestor of two species existed.
	b)		15 million years ago	1	Remember, the common ancestor existed at the most recent branching of the groups.
	c)		Individual genomes can reveal likelihood/risk of genetic disease = **1** So that different lifestyle advice/drug treatment can be offered = **1**	2	Each person's genome is slightly different, so it is possible that in the future treatments can be personalised based on known genetic components of disease.
5	a)		Endothelium	1	Thin layer of cells separating the lumen from the vessel walls.
	b)		**Role**: prevent backflow of blood = **1** **Explanation**: blood in veins is at (very) low pressure **AND** working against gravity when standing = **1**	2	During diastole, blood still needs to pass along veins. Valves are needed as the blood is flowing back to the heart at low pressure and generally against the force of gravity. Remember not to say that valves keep blood flowing in one direction – they are passive and simply prevent backflow when pressure drops.
	c)	(i)	A blood clot which occurs within a vein (deep in the body tissues)	1	DVT is a peripheral vascular disorder.
		(ii)	Slows or stops the passage of blood through the vein	1	Pain is experienced in the leg muscle due to limited supply of oxygen.
6	a)	(i)	13.6 μl/ml	1	Read up from 10 minutes using a ruler then use the ruler to read across to the right Y axis.
		(ii)	96.8 mg/100 ml	1	Read across from the right Y axis to the dotted line then read up to the glucose line and finally across to the Y axis value on the left-hand side of the graph.
	b)		Adrenaline causes release of glucose from stored glycogen = **1** Released glucose can be used for energy during the jog = **1**	2	Adrenaline can be released from the adrenal gland by sympathetic fibres of the autonomic nervous system.
	c)		Receptors on cells are not sensitive to insulin so do not take in glucose and convert it to glycogen	1	Remember, type 1 diabetes involves lack of insulin but type 2 involves lack of receptor sensitivity.

Question			Expected answer	Mark	Commentary with hints and tips
7	a)		Mast cell	1	Mast cells are scattered throughout the skin and can release histamine following activation.
	b)		Vasodilation = **1** Increased permeability of capillaries = **1**	2	Vasodilation is the widening of blood vessel, allowing more blood cells into an area; increased permeability of capillaries allows easier release of defence chemicals into an area.
	c)		Cytokines = **1** Stimulate activity of lymphocytes/immune response = **1**	2	Although cytokines are released in response to non-specific damage, they do activate specific immunity.
8	a)		Items become displaced because STM has a limited span **OR** Items decay because STM has a limited duration/time it retains information	1	Short-term memory is limited to only a few items and these can be discarded by decay or displaced by new items entering.
	b)	(i)	Rehearsal **OR** organisation	1	Remember **ROE** – **R**ehearsal, **O**rganisation and **E**laboration – methods which encourage transfer of items to the long-term memory.
		(ii)	Elaborative encoding involves additional/meaningful information (to provide context for memory)	1	In elaboration, extra information is added to the information which is to be remembered – for example, existing memories of baking a cake can help to bring an ingredients list for the cake into long-term memory.
	c)		Failure of emotional or spatial memories	1	Different types of memories are stored in different places in the brain.
9	a)	(i)	16 units	1	Read up from 15 nM on the X axis and count the difference between the two drugs.
		(ii)	25%	1	Use the key to be sure that you use the morphine graph; select the electrical response at 5 nM = 20 and at 10 nM = 25, then subtract = 5; 5 divided by 20 × 100 = 25%.
		(iii)	From 0–5 nM increases from 0 to 20 units = **1** From 5–25 nM increases from 20 to 37 units = **1**	2	Make sure you use values to describe the data – you must use values from both axes to score the marks; only general trends need to be picked out.
		(iv)	39 units	1	Extend the graph line on its current trend and read off from the electrical response.
	b)		6.0 units	1	Read up from 5 nM to the morphine line on Graph 1 = 12 units. Next read up from 5 nM of the experimental drug in Graph 2 = 50% of the maximum activity. So, 50% of 12 = 6.
	c)		8.5 nM	1	Tricky! Reduction of 70% means the response is still at 30% of the original; read across from 30% to the drug line and down to the X axis to read 8.5 nM.

Question			Expected answer	Mark	Commentary with hints and tips
10	a)	(i)	Non-verbal communication	1	Non-verbal communication does not involve language, either written or spoken – there is a symbol and an image of a handshake.
		(ii)	Allows communication with babies **OR** Adds meaning to verbal communication **OR** Language barriers to be overcome **OR** Can signal emotions	1	The symbol for no smoking can be understood regardless of the language a person speaks; a handshake adds meaning to interpersonal communication.
	b)	(i)	Creates a motor memory/pathway	1	Repeated use of a motor pathway helps to establish a motor memory, allowing further repeats of an action without conscious thought.
		(ii)	Child progresses by trial and error learning = **1** Rewarding successful behaviour causes it to be reinforced = **1**	2	Shaping allows training to occur by rewarding desired behaviour.
		(iii)	Generalisation	1	This is where a learned behaviour is applied to situations without discrimination.
11	a)	(i)	Antigens	1	Vaccines contain antigens which have been rendered harmless but which can still produce an immune response.
		(ii)	B lymphocyte	1	Receptors on B lymphocytes produce specific antibodies in response to specific antigens.
		(iii)	The antibodies only recognise the antigen from the polio virus.	1	There are different antibodies for all the different antigens.
	b)		Cells produce enzymes that cause self-destruction	1	Apoptosis is cell suicide. Infected cells are sacrificed to prevent them infecting other cells.
12	a)		5%	1	Increase = 84 – 80 = 4. Percentage increase = increase starting value × 100. So, $\frac{4}{80}$ × 100 = 5%.
	b)	(i)	Blood pressure after taking a caffeine drink	1	Dependent variables are affected by changing the independent variable. **DD** = **D**ependent variable refers to **D**ata produced (results).
		(ii)	Other drinks/food taken (before or after) **OR** Concentration of energy drink **OR** Activities carried out during the hour	1	Any variable that could affect the results should be controlled.

Question			Expected answer	Mark	Commentary with hints and tips
	c)		Another similar group of volunteers who were treated in the same way but were not given caffeine	1	The control proves that the independent variable is causing changes to the dependent variable.
	d)		Scales and labels from table = **1** Stacked bars accurately plotted = **1**	2	Make sure your chart takes up more than half of the graph paper, and that the axes are both labelled with units where appropriate.
	e)	(i)	Caffeine increases systolic/ diastolic BP	1	This is a summary of what the results show.
		(ii)	Ages/genders/weights of volunteers not taken into account	1	If the sample is biased for some reason, the conclusions cannot be valid.
13			**Individual** Good hygiene Care in sexual health Appropriate handling/storage of food *Any 2* **Community** Quality water supply Safe food webs Appropriate waste disposal systems *Any 2*	1 1 1 2 1 1 1 2	The points here are probably quite easy to hit because they are part of the everyday practices we all try to follow – a list in your answer is fine.
			Total	4	
14	A		1 Double helix. 2 Two strands of nucleotides. 3 Nucleotide = sugar + phosphate + base. 4 Sugar–phosphate backbone. 5 Complementary base pairs **OR** A with T and G with C. 6 Held by hydrogen bonds. 7 Antiparallel strands **OR** strands run in opposite directions. *Any 5* 8 Strand separates. 9 Primers bind. 10 DNA polymerase adds complementary bases/ nucleotides /continuously on one/the lead strand.	1 1 1 1 1 1 1 5 1 1 1	In longer ER questions, it is vital to use the language which is in the CAS – this is the key to scoring marks. Use the reference in the student margin to find the CAS entry and the Key Points list in HTP. Having a few titles for each unit well learned is a good exam revision technique.

Question			Expected answer	Mark	Commentary with hints and tips
			11 Other strand synthesised in fragments.	1	
			12 Fragments joined with ligase.	1	
			Any 4	4	
			Total	9	
		B	**1** Sets of enzyme-controlled reactions.	1	
			2 Some enzymes work as multi-enzyme complexes/in groups.	1	
			3 Some reactions are reversible.	1	
			4 Some reactions have alternative pathways.	1	
			5 Enzymes specific to their reactions **OR** have active sites complementary in shape to substrate.	1	
			6 Lower activation energy needed to start a reaction.	1	
			7 Binds to substrate by induced fit.	1	
			8 Have high affinity for substrates but low affinity for products.	1	
			9 Can be reused following a reaction.	1	
			10 Have optimum temperature/pH.	1	
			11 Denatured by high temperatures/extremes of pH.	1	
			12 Can be affected by inhibitors.	1	
			Any 9	9	

Extended Response Questions

Unit 1: Human Cells

Key Area	Question		Expected answer		Mark	Student margin
1.1	1	(i)	1	Stem cells can continue to divide.	1	**CAS** page 8
			2	Can differentiate into specialised cells.	1	**HTP** page 1
			3	Embryonic stem cells can become any kind of cell.	1	
			4	Adult stem cells can become more limited types.	1	
			5	Adult stem cells divide and differentiate to replenish cells which need to be replaced.	1	
			6	Adult stem cells in bone marrow give rise to various types of blood cell.	1	
			Any 5		5	
		(ii)	7	Stem cells can be used as model cells to study how diseases develop.	1	
			8	Stem cells can be used for drug testing.	1	
			9	Stem cells can be used in the repair of damaged tissues.	1	
			10	Stem cells can be used in the repair of diseased tissue.	1	
			Any 3		3	
			Total		8	
1.2	2	(i)	1	Double-stranded helix.	1	**CAS** page 9
			2	Strands made up of nucleotides.	1	**HTP** page 10
			3	Nucleotide composed of deoxyribose, phosphate and base.	1	
			4	Each strand has a sugar–phosphate backbone.	1	
			5	Strands connected through bases by H bonds.	1	
			6	Bases complementary/A pairs with T and G pairs with C.	1	
			7	Strands antiparallel/run in opposite directions.	1	
			8	Each strand has phosphate at 5′ end and sugar at 3′ end.	1	
			Any 5		5	
		(ii)	9	Double helix (uncoils and) unzips.	1	
			10	Primers add on to template strands.	1	
			11	Primers allow DNA polymerase/enzyme to bind.	1	
			12	DNA polymerase adds complementary DNA nucleotide to templates.	1	
			13	One/lead strand replicated continuously.	1	
			14	The other/lag strand replicated in fragments.	1	
			15	Fragments joined by ligase.	1	
			Any 4		4	
			Total		9	

Key Area	Question		Expected answer	Mark	Student margin
1.3	3	(i)	1 DNA unwinds and unzips.	1	**CAS** page 9
			2 RNA polymerase adds complementary RNA nucleotides.	1	**HTP** page 16
			3 (To make a) primary transcript.	1	
			4 Introns removed.	1	
			5 Exons spliced to make mRNA.	1	
			Any 4	4	
		(ii)	6 mRNA goes to ribosome.	1	
			7 tRNA carries specific amino acids.	1	
			8 Anti-codons on tRNA aligned with codons on mRNA.	1	
			9 Amino acids aligned in correct sequence.	1	
			10 Amino acids linked by peptide bonds.	1	
			Any 4	4	
			Total	**8**	
1.4	4		1 Substitution.	1	**CAS** page 9
			2 Involves swapping one nucleotide for another.	1	**HTP** page 23
			3 Substitutions can be missense, in which a change in one codon results in a different amino acid being used.	1	
			4 Substitutions can be nonsense, in which a codon is changed to a stop codon making the protein shorter.	1	
			5 Substitutions give minor changes to protein structure.	1	
			6 Deletion.	1	
			7 Involves the removal of a nucleotide from the sequence.	1	
			8 Insertion.	1	
			9 Involves the addition of a nucleotide to the sequence.	1	
			10 Deletion/insertion give frameshift effects to amino acid sequence in the protein.	1	
			11 Frameshift/deletion/insertion give major changes to protein structure.	1	
			Any 7	7	
	5	(i)	1 Substitution/missense mutation results in protein with slightly altered structure.	1	**CAS** page 9
			2 Altered protein cannot function normally.	1	**HTP** page 23
			3 Failure of function has an impact on health/example/ sickle cell disease.	1	
			4 Deletion/insertion/nonsense mutation results in no/ much altered protein	1	
			5 Are likely to be lethal.	1	
			Any 3	3	
		(ii)	6 Deletion involves loss of part of a chromosome.	1	
			7 Duplication involves repeat sections of a chromosome.	1	
			8 Translocation involves part of a chromosome being attached to another chromosome.	1	
			9 The substantial changes involved often make these mutations lethal.	1	
			Any 3	3	
			Total	**6**	

Key Area	Question		Expected answer	Mark	Student margin
1.5	6		**1** DNA sample treated with an array of DNA probes.	1	**CAS** page 10
			2 Specific sequences detected by the probes.	1	**HTP** page 29
			3 Fluorescent labelling allows the detection under UV light of the identified sequences.	1	
			4 Sequences can be separated (by electrophoresis) to give a DNA profile.	1	
			5 Individuals vary in the numbers of sequences repeats their DNA contains.	1	
			6 Profiles are unique to individuals.	1	
			7 Allows identification of individuals from their DNA in forensics.	1	
			8 Allow parents of a child to be identified.	1	
			Any 4 from 1–5 and Any 2 from 6–8	6	
1.6	7		**1** Enzyme activity depends on the flexible/dynamic shape of enzyme molecules.	1	**CAS** page 10
			2 Substrate has an affinity for the active site.	1	**HTP** page 35
			3 Induced fit.	1	
			4 Active site orientates the reactants.	1	
			5 Enzymes lower the activation energy.	1	
			6 Products have a low affinity for the active site.	1	
			7 Substrate and product concentration affects the direction and rate of reactions.	1	
			OR		
			Increasing the substrate concentration increases/ speeds up/drives forward the rate of the reaction.	1	
			8 Enzymes act in groups/multi-enzyme complex.	1	
			Any 6	6	
			9 In competitive inhibition the inhibitor resembles the substrate molecule/blocks the active site.	1	
			10 Inhibition is reduced by increase in substrate concentration.	1	
			11 Effects are reversible.	1	
			12 In non-competitive inhibition the shape of the active site is changed.	1	
			13 Effects are irreversible **OR** inhibitors bind but not at the active site.	1	
			14 In end-product/feedback inhibition, end product inhibits an enzyme early in a metabolic pathway.	1	
			Any 4	4	
			Total	10	

Key Area	Question		Expected answer	Mark	Student margin
	8		1 Anabolic pathways require energy.	1	**CAS** page 10
			2 Catabolic pathways release energy.	1	**HTP** page 35
			3 Reversible and irreversible pathways.	1	
			4 Regulation by intra- and extracellular molecules.	1	
			5 Enzymes can work in groups/multi enzyme complexes.	1	
			6 Activation energy lowered by enzymes.	1	
			7 Enzymes have affinity for substrate but less for product molecules.	1	
			8 Induced fit of enzymes to substrates.	1	
			9 Fit occurs at active site.	1	
			10 Enzyme reaction rate can be reduced by inhibitors.	1	
			11 Competitive inhibitors block active sites.	1	
			12 Non-competitive inhibitors bind to other regions of enzyme molecule.	1	
			13 Feedback/end-product inhibition.	1	
			Any 9	9	
1.7	9	(i)	1 Glycolysis is the breakdown of glucose to pyruvate.	1	**CAS** page 10
			2 ATP molecules are used to phosphorylate intermediates in glycolysis.	1	**HTP** page 42
			3 An energy investment phase.	1	
			4 ATP molecules are produced/generated/made in a pay off stage.	1	
			Any 3	3	
		(ii)	5 If oxygen is available/in aerobic conditions pyruvate progresses to the citric acid cycle.	1	
			6 Pyruvate is converted/broken down to an acetyl group.	1	
			7 Acetyl group combines with coenzyme A.	1	
			8 Acetyl (coenzyme A) combines with oxaloacetate to form citrate.	1	
			9 Citric acid cycle is enzyme controlled/involves dehydrogenases.	1	
			10 ATP generated/synthesised/produced/released at substrate level in the citric acid cycle.	1	
			11 Carbon dioxide is released from the citric acid cycle.	1	
			12 Oxaloacetate is regenerated.	1	
			13 NAD/NADH/$NADH_2$/FAD/FADH/$FADH_2$ transports electrons/transports hydrogen ions to the electron transport chain.	1	
			Any 6	6	
			Total	9	

Key Area	Question		Expected answer	Mark	Student margin
	10		1 Electron transport chain takes place on the inner membrane of the mitochondria/cristae.	1	**CAS** page 10 **HTP** page 42
			2 Electron transport chain is a collection of proteins attached to a membrane.	1	
			3 NADH and $FADH_2$ release high-energy electrons to the electron transport chain on the inner mitochondrial membrane.	1	
			4 Electrons pass down the chain of electron acceptors, releasing their energy.	1	
			5 Energy is used to pump hydrogen ions (H^+) across the inner mitochondrial membrane.	1	
			6 Return flow of the hydrogen ions (H^+) back into the matrix drives the enzyme ATP synthase.	1	
			7 Synthesis of ATP from ADP + P_i.	1	
			8 This stage produces most of the ATP generated by cellular respiration.	1	
			9 Final electron acceptor is oxygen.	1	
			10 Oxygen combines with hydrogen ions and electrons to form water.	1	
			Any 8	8	
	11	(i)	1 ATP produced by phosphorylation/when P_i added to ADP.	1	**CAS** page 10 **HTP** page 42
			2 Acts as a source of immediate energy for cells **OR** transfers energy within cells.	1	
			3 Made during respiration.	1	
			4 Used up during energy-requiring processes/muscle contraction/protein synthesis.	1	
			5 Mass in cell remains constant.	1	
			Any 4	4	
		(ii)	6 Substrates are used instead of/as an alternative to glucose/when glucose not available.	1	
			7 Examples from starch/glycogen/other sugars/amino acids/fats.	1	
			8 Glycogen is a storage carbohydrate from liver/muscles.	1	
			9 Glycogen is used between meals.	1	
			10 Amino acids can be released from body bulk protein.	1	
			11 These amino acids can be used during extreme starvation.	1	
			12 Other sugars/amino acids can enter respiration pathways/glycolysis/citric acid cycle.	1	
			Any 4	4	
			Total	8	

Key Area	Question		Expected answer	Mark	Student margin
1.8	12	(i)	1 Slow twitch muscle fibres contract slowly but maintain contractions for a long time.	1	**CAS** page 11 **HTP** page 48
			2 They rely on aerobic respiration (to generate ATP).	1	
			3 They have many mitochondria/a large blood supply/a high concentration of myoglobin.	1	
			4 Their (main) storage fuel/energy source is fats.	1	
			5 Good for endurance activities/example.	1	
			Any 3	3	
		(ii)	6 Fast twitch muscle fibres contract quickly but cannot maintain contractions for a long time.	1	
			7 They generate ATP through glycolysis.	1	
			8 They have few mitochondria and a low blood supply.	1	
			9 Their (main) storage fuels/energy sources are glycogen and creatine phosphate.	1	
			10 Good for short bursts of intense activity/example.	1	
			Any 3	3	
			Total	6	
	13	(i)	1 During exercise (muscles) do not receive enough oxygen for (aerobic) respiration/the electron transport chain.	1	**CAS** page 11 **HTP** page 48
			2 Pyruvate/pyruvic acid is converted to lactic acid.	1	
			3 This involves the transfer of hydrogen from NADH (produced during glycolysis).	1	
			4 This regenerates the NAD needed to maintain ATP production by glycolysis.	1	
			5 Lactic acid builds up (in muscles) causing fatigue/an oxygen debt.	1	
			6 (When exercise stops) lactic acid is converted back into pyruvate/pyruvic acid/glucose (in the liver).	1	
			Any 4	4	
		(ii)	7 Contract slowly but maintain contractions for a long time.	1	
			8 They rely on aerobic respiration (to generate ATP).	1	
			9 They have many mitochondria/a large blood supply/a high concentration of myoglobin.	1	
			10 Their (main) storage fuel/energy source is fats.	1	
			Any 3	3	
		(iii)	11 Contract quickly but cannot maintain contractions for a long time.	1	
			12 They generate ATP through glycolysis.	1	
			13 They have few mitochondria and a low blood supply.	1	
			14 Their (main) storage fuels/energy sources are glycogen and creatine phosphate.	1	
			15 Examples given of appropriate activities which use slow twitch and fast twitch muscle fibres, e.g. long-distance running, cycling or cross-country skiing for slow twitch and sprinting or weightlifting for fast twitch.	1	
			Allocate the examples in either section (ii) or (iii)		
			Any 3	3	
			Total	10	

Unit 2: Physiology and Health

Key Area	Question	Expected answer	Mark	Student margin
2.1	14	1 Ova produced/matured in the ovaries.	1	**CAS** page 11
		2 Ova develop inside Graafian follicles.	1	**HTP** page 64
		3 Release of ova during ovulation.	1	
		4 Ovaries release oestrogen.	1	
		5 Ova move along oviducts/fallopian tubes (towards the uterus).	1	
		6 Fertilisation occurs in the oviduct.	1	
		7 To produce a zygote.	1	
		8 Zygote develops into a blastocyst.	1	
		9 Blastocyst implants into the endometrium/uterus lining.	1	
		10 Embryo completes development within uterus.	1	
		Any 8	8	
2.2	15	1 FSH stimulates the maturation of a follicle surrounding the ovum and the production of the oestrogen by the follicle.	1	**CAS** page 11
		2 High levels of oestrogen stimulate the secretion of LH by the pituitary gland.	1	**HTP** page 68
		3 LH stimulates the corpus luteum to secrete progesterone.	1	
		4 High levels of oestrogen and progesterone inhibit the secretion of FSH and LH by the pituitary gland.	1	
		5 This is an example of negative feedback control.	1	
		6 If fertilisation does not occur, this results in a drop in LH levels.	1	
		7 This causes the corpus luteum to break down.	1	
		8 Which in turn causes a decrease in progesterone and oestrogen levels.	1	
		Any 6	6	
	16	1 Pituitary gland produces FSH.	1	**CAS** page 11
		2 FSH promotes sperm production.	1	**HTP** page 68
		3 Sperm are produced in the seminiferous tubules.	1	
		4 Pituitary gland produces ICSH.	1	
		5 LH stimulates testosterone production in the interstitial cells.	1	
		6 Testosterone stimulates sperm production.	1	
		7 Testosterone influences the production of semen/ prostate gland/seminal vesicles.	1	
		8 Higher levels of testosterone inhibit ICSH/FSH.	1	
		9 This is negative feedback.	1	
		10 This ensures that levels of testosterone are kept within the normal range/constant.	1	
		Any 9	9	

Key Area	Question		Expected answer	Mark	Student margin
	17		1 Cycle starts with menstruation.	1	**CAS** page 11
			2 This involves the breakdown of the lining of the uterus/ endometrium.	1	**HTP** page 68
			3 Pituitary gland secretes FSH.	1	
			4 FSH stimulates growth of a follicle.	1	
			5 Follicle/ovary produces oestrogen.	1	
			6 Oestrogen stimulates the repair of the endometrium/ uterus lining.	1	
			7 Oestrogen also stimulates the production of LH.	1	
			8 LH is produced by the pituitary gland.	1	
			9 LH brings about ovulation.	1	
			10 Rising levels of oestrogen inhibit FSH production.	1	
			11 This is negative feedback.	1	
			Any 9	9	
	18	(i)	1 Pituitary gland secretes/produces FSH/LH.	1	**CAS** page 11
			2 FSH stimulates growth of follicle (in the ovary).	1	**HTP** page 68
			3 Follicle/ovary produces oestrogen.	1	
			4 Oestrogen stimulates/repairs the endometrium/uterus lining.	1	
			5 Oestrogen stimulates production of LH.	1	
			6 LH (surge) brings about ovulation/release of the egg.	1	
			7 Rising/high levels of oestrogen inhibit FSH production.	1	
			8 This is negative feedback.	1	
			Any 6	6	
		(ii)	9 The follicle develops into the corpus luteum.	1	
			10 Corpus luteum secretes progesterone (and oestrogen).	1	
			11 Progesterone maintains/increases/thickens the endometrium/uterus lining.	1	
			12 Progesterone/oestrogen inhibits FSH/LH production.	1	
			(Point 8 may be awarded here if linked to Point 12.)		
			13 Progesterone/oestrogen levels decrease towards the end of the cycle.	1	
			14 This/corpus luteum degeneration triggers menstruation/breakdown of the endometrium.	1	
			Any 4	4	
			Total	10	

Key Area	Question		Expected answer	Mark	Student margin
2.3	19		**1** Failure to ovulate.	1	**CAS** page 11
			2 Cause: hormone imbalance/lack of hormones (FSH and LH)/prolonged use of contraceptive pill; health reasons: anorexia/obesity/drug misuse/smoking/stress/poor diet.	1	**HTP** page 74
			3 Treatment: ovulatory (fertility) drugs/hormone treatment/donor egg GIFT (gamete intrafallopian tube transfer)/improved lifestyle.	1	
			4 Blockage/spasm of uterine.	1	
			5 Cause: endometriosis/STD (sexually transmitted disease)/infection/cancer.	1	
			6 Treatment: surgery/laser treatment/anti-spasmodic drugs/IVF/fertilisation outside woman's body/in glass/in dish.	1	
			7 Failure of implantation.	1	
			8 Cause: hormone imbalance.	1	
			9 Treatment: ovulatory/fertility drugs.	1	
			Total	9	
2.4	20		**1** Mother's blood pressure/blood type/blood tests/urine tests/general health check.	1	**CAS** page 12
			2 Ultrasound (imaging/scan).	1	**HTP** page 83
			3 Dating scan/scan at 8–14 weeks is used to determine stage of pregnancy/due date.	1	
			4 Anomaly scan/scan at 18–20 weeks for serious physical problems.	1	
			5 Biochemical/chemical tests detect (physiological) changes of pregnancy.	1	
			6 Marker chemicals/named chemical can indicate medical conditions/can give a false positive result.	1	
			7 Diagnostic/further testing can follow from routine testing/named test.	1	
			8 Amniocentesis/cells from amniotic fluid used to produce karyotype/to test for Down syndrome/chromosome abnormalities.	1	
			9 Chorionic villus sampling/CVS – cells from placenta/chorion used to produce karyotype/to test for Down syndrome/chromosome abnormalities.	1	
			10 CVS carried out earlier in pregnancy than amniocentesis allows immediate karyotyping.	1	
			11 CVS has higher risk of miscarriage.	1	
			12 Rhesus antibody testing described (for sensitisation of Rh- mother by Rh+ antigens).	1	
			Any 9	9	

Key Area	Question		Expected answer	Mark	Student margin
2.5	21		**1** Arteries carry blood away from the heart.	1	**CAS** page 12
			2 Blood is pumped through arteries at a high pressure.	1	**HTP** page 91
			3 Arteries have an outer layer containing elastic fibres.	1	
			4 A thick middle layer containing smooth muscle with more elastic fibres.	1	
			5 Relatively narrow lumen.	1	
			6 Elastic walls of the arteries stretch and recoil to accommodate the surge of blood pressure after each contraction of the heart.	1	
			Any 4	4	
			7 Veins carry blood towards the heart.	1	
			8 Veins have an outer layer of connective tissue containing elastic fibres.	1	
			9 Thinner muscular wall than arteries.	1	
			10 The lumen of a vein is wider than that of an artery.	1	
			11 Valves are present in veins to prevent the back flow of blood.	1	
			12 Valves needed as the blood is flowing back to the heart at low pressure.	1	
			Any 4	4	
			13 Capillary walls are only one cell thick.	1	
			14 Allows quick/efficient exchange of materials/ substances with tissues.	1	
			Any 1	1	
			Total	9	
2.6	22	(i)	**1** Pacemaker/SAN contains autorhythmic cells/is where the heart beat originates/is found in the right atrium.	1	**CAS** page 12
			2 Impulse/wave of excitation spreads across the atria/ cause the atria to contract/cause atrial systole.	1	**HTP** page 97
			3 (Impulses) reach/stimulate the atrioventricular node/AVN.	1	
			4 AVN found at junction of atria and ventricles/at base of atria.	1	
			5 Impulses from AVN spread through ventricles.	1	
			6 (Cause) contraction of ventricles/ventricular systole.	1	
			7 (This is followed by) relaxation/resting/diastolic phase/diastole.	1	
			Any 5	5	
		(ii)	**8** Medulla controls the cardiac cycle/regulates the SAN.	1	
			9 Autonomic nervous system (carries impulses to heart).	1	
			10 Sympathetic nerve speeds up the heart rate.	1	
			11 Sympathetic nerve releases noradrenaline/ norepinephrine.	1	
			12 Parasympathetic nerve slows down the heart rate.	1	
			13 Parasympathetic nerve releases acetylcholine.	1	
			14 Sympathetic and parasympathetic systems are antagonistic to each other.	1	
			Any 5	5	
			Total	10	

Key Area	Question		Expected answer	Mark	Student margin
2.7	23		**1** Endothelium is damaged.	1	**CAS** page 13
			2 Clotting factors are released.	1	**HTP** page 106
			3 Prothrombin (enzyme) is converted/activated/changed into thrombin.	1	
			4 Fibrinogen is converted into fibrin (by thrombin).	1	
			5 Fibrin/threads form a meshwork (that seals the wound).	1	
			6 Clot/thrombus formed may break loose, forming an embolus.	1	
			7 Clot/thrombus may lead to a heart attack/stroke.	1	
			Any 6	6	
2.8	24		**1** Negative feedback maintains constant internal conditions in the body/homeostasis.	1	**CAS** page 13
			2 A change from the normal level/set point is detected.	1	**HTP** page 112
			3 Corrective mechanism is switched on/activated.	1	
			4 When condition returns to its normal level/set point, corrective mechanism is switched off.	1	
			Any 2	2	
			5 Blood sugar/glucose concentration/level detected by the pancreas/pancreatic receptors.	1	
			6 If blood glucose concentration increases, (more) insulin is released.	1	
			7 Insulin increases permeability of cells to glucose OR insulin increases uptake of glucose by cells.	1	
			8 Liver/muscle cells convert glucose to glycogen OR glucose converted to glycogen and stored in liver/muscle.	1	
			9 Blood glucose concentration returns to its normal/set point.	1	
			10 If blood glucose concentration decreases, (more) glucagon is released.	1	
			11 Glucagon causes conversion of glycogen to glucose.	1	
			12 Glucose released into blood.	1	
			13 Blood glucose concentration returns to normal/set point.	1	
			Any 7	7	
			Total	9	

Unit 3: Neurobiology and Communication

Key Area	Question		Expected answer	Mark	Student margin
3.1	25		1 ANS works automatically/without conscious control **OR** controls involuntary responses.	1	**CAS** page 13 **HTP** page 135
			2 Impulses originate in the medulla (region of the brain).	1	
			3 Made up of sympathetic and parasympathetic systems/fibres.	1	
			4 These two systems act antagonistically/description.	1	
			5 Sympathetic system prepares the body for fight or flight.	1	
			6 Parasympathetic system prepares the body for resting and digesting.	1	
			7 Correct description of the effect of the ANS in controlling heart rate.	1	
			8 Correct description of the effect of the ANS in controlling breathing rate.	1	
			9 Correct description of the effect of the ANS in controlling peristalsis.	1	
			10 Correct description of the effect of the ANS in controlling intestinal secretions.	1	
			Any 8	8	
3.2	26	(i)	1 Lasts a few seconds.	1	**CAS** page 14 **HTP** page 140
			2 All visual and auditory input retained.	1	
			3 Passed into STM.	1	
			Any 2	2	
		(ii)	4 Short span.	1	
			5 Affected by serial position effect.	1	
			6 Maintained by rehearsal.	1	
			7 Items displaced/undergo decay.	1	
			8 Improved by chunking.	1	
			Any 3	3	
		(iii)	9 Items transferred from STM.	1	
			10 By rehearsal.	1	
			11 By organisation.	1	
			12 By elaboration.	1	
			13 Information encoded by shallow or elaborative means.	1	
			14 Retrieval aided by contextual cues.	1	
			Any 4	4	
			Total	9	

Key Area	Question		Expected answer	Mark	Student margin
3.3	27	(i)	**1** Cell body with nucleus.	1	**CAS** page 14
			2 Fibres called axons carry impulses away from cell body.	1	**HTP** page 149
			3 Fibres called dendrites carry impulses to cell body.	1	
			4 Some fibres are myelinated.	1	
			5 Sensory neurons carry impulses from sense organs to CNS.	1	
			6 Inter-neurons connect other neurons in CNS.	1	
			7 Motor neurons carry impulses from CNS to muscles or gland.	1	
			Any 5	5	
		(ii)	**8** Support neurons.	1	
			9 Make myelin sheath.	1	
			10 Keep environment homeostatic.	1	
			11 Clear debris/phagocytosis.	1	
			Any 3	3	
			Total	8	
	28	(i)	**1** Synapse/synaptic cleft is the junction/gap between neurons/nerve cells **OR** labelled diagram.	1	**CAS** page 14
			2 Neurotransmitters are stored in/released from vesicles.	1	**HTP** page 149
			3 Neurotransmitters are released on arrival of impulse.	1	
			4 Neurotransmitters diffuse across the gap.	1	
			5 Neurotransmitters bind with/reach receptors.	1	
			6 Threshold/minimum number of neurotransmitters is needed (for the impulse to continue).	1	
			7 Neurotransmitters are removed by enzymes and reuptake/reabsorption.	1	
			8 Neurotransmitters must be removed to prevent continuous stimulation.	1	
			9 Any named neurotransmitter from – acetylcholine, noradrenaline, dopamine, endorphins.	1	
			Any 5	5	
		(ii)	**10** Converging pathway has several neurones linked to one neurone. **OR** Labelled diagram but must show direction of impulse.	1	
			11 This increases the neurotransmitter concentration/chances of impulse.	1	
			12 Generation/sensitivity to excitory or inhibitory signals.	1	
			13 Diverging pathway has one neurone linked to several neurones. **OR** Labelled diagram but must show direction of impulse.	1	
			14 This means that impulses are sent to/influence several destinations at the same time.	1	

Key Area	Question		Expected answer	Mark	Student margin
			15 Reverberating pathways – neurones later in pathway synapse/link with neurones earlier in the pathway.	1	
			16 New neural pathways can bypass areas of brain damage/create new responses/suppress reflexes/create plasticity.	1	
			Any 4	4	
			Total	9	
3.4	29	(i)	**1** Communication by body language/posture.	1	**CAS** page 15
			2 Facial expression/gestures.	1	**HTP** page 158
			3 Signals attitude and emotion.	1	
			4 Can support verbal communication.	1	
			Any 3	3	
		(ii)	**5** Communication by written/spoken word/example.	1	
			6 Another example.	1	
			7 (Used to) transmit knowledge	1	
			8 (and) culture.	1	
			9 (Allows) social evolution.	1	
			Any 4	4	
			Total	7	
	30	(i)	**1** Social facilitation is increased performance.	1	**CAS** page 15
			2 In presence of an audience/competitors.	1	**HTP** page 158
			3 Identification is the adoption of the behaviours/beliefs.	1	
			4 Of a role model/admired person.	1	
			Any 3	3	
		(ii)	**5** De-individuation is loss of personal responsibility for actions.	1	
			6 And passing it on to other members of a group.	1	
			7 Internalisation is the adoption of the behaviours/beliefs of an other.	1	
			8 Through persuasion.	1	
			Any 3	3	
			Total	6	

Unit 4: Immunology and Public Health

Key Area	Question		Expected answer	Mark	Student margin
4.1	31		1 Intact skin prevents the entry of pathogens/is a physical barrier.	1	**CAS** page 15 **HTP** page 171
			2 Epithelial cells (in cavity linings) produce (protective chemical) secretions.	1	
			3 Description of one non-specific defence from mucus in windpipe/acid in stomach/lysozyme or antibacterial substances in tears/coughing or sneezing/blood clotting.	1	
			4 Inflammatory response is caused by the release of histamine from mast cells.	1	
			5 Vasodilation/increased capillary permeability/increased blood flow (occurs).	1	
			6 Increased blood flow/secretion of cytokines results in the accumulation of phagocytes.	1	
			7 Results in the delivery of antimicrobial proteins/clotting elements to the site.	1	
			8 Phagocytes recognise surface antigens/protein markers on pathogens.	1	
			9 They then destroy the pathogen by engulfing it/by phagocytosis.	1	
			10 Natural killer (NK) cells induce the pathogen to destroy itself/apoptosis.	1	
			11 Cause pathogen to produce digestive/self-destructive enzymes/phagocytes/NK cells release cytokines that stimulate the (specific) immune response.	1	
			Any 9	9	
4.2	32	(i)	1 Responds to specific antigens by producing a clone.	1	**CAS** page 16 **HTP** page 175
			2 B lymphocytes activated by antigen presenting cells/T cells.	1	
			3 B lymphocytes produce antibodies.	1	
			4 Antibodies released into blood or lymph and bind to specific antigen.	1	
			5 Antigens rendered harmless.	1	
			Any 4	4	
		(ii)	6 Respond to specific antigens by producing a clone.	1	
			7 Have surface protein which allows them to distinguish between self and foreign antigens.	1	
			8 One group induces apoptosis in infected cells.	1	
			9 One group secretes cytokines to activate B cells and phagocytes.	1	
			Any 3	3	
			Total	7	

Key Area	Question		Expected answer	Mark	Student margin
	33		1 Active immunity is when the body makes antibodies in response to an infection/pathogen/disease.	1	**CAS** page 16 **HTP** page 175
			2 Invading pathogens have antigens (on their surface).	1	
			3 Lymphocytes recognise foreign/non-self antigens (on the invading pathogen).	1	
			4 B lymphocytes produce antibodies.	1	
			5 Antibodies are specific/have receptor sites which bind/attach to foreign antigens.	1	
			6 T lymphocytes kill the infected cell/produce chemicals that destroy microbes.	1	
			7 Following an infection memory cells are produced/remain in the body.	1	
			8 These detect a reinvading microbe and destroy it (before it can cause infection).	1	
			9 This (secondary) response is faster/stronger (than the primary response).	1	
			Any 7	7	
4.3	34		1 Sporadic.	1	**CAS** page 16 **HTP** page 181
			2 Occasional occurrence in an area.	1	
			3 Endemic.	1	
			4 Regular occurrence in an area.	1	
			5 Epidemic.	1	
			6 High number of cases in an area.	1	
			7 Pandemic.	1	
			8 An epidemic on a global scale.	1	
			Any 6 must match	6	
	35	(i)	1 Diseases are caused by pathogens, e.g. viruses, bacteria, fungi, protozoa, e.g. of any multicellular organism.	2	**CAS** page 16 **HTP** page 181
			Any 2, 1 mark each		
			2 Diseases are transmitted by direct physical contact/indirect contact/bodily fluids/inhaled air/droplets in air (coughing/sneezing).	1	
			3 Diseases are transmitted by infected food/water.	1	
			4 Diseases are transmitted by animal vectors.	1	
			5 One example of a named disease and how it is spread.	1	
			Any 3	3	
		(ii)	6 Vaccination or immunisation/drug therapy/antibiotic use/antiviral drugs/antiseptics/disinfectants.	2	
			Any 2, 1 mark each		
			7 Maintaining clean water/sanitation (separating sewage and drinking water)/quarantine **OR** description.	1	
			8 Good (personal) hygiene/care in sexual health/education about hygiene.	1	
			9 Safe storage/handling of food.	1	
			10 Control of vectors, e.g. use of pesticides.	1	
			Any 3	3	

Key Area	Question		Expected answer	Mark	Student margin
		(iii)	11 Sporadic – disease occurs occasionally.	1	
			12 Endemic – regular cases occur in an area or disease is typical of an area.	1	
			13 Epidemic – (unusually) high number of cases in an area.	1	
			14 Pandemic – global epidemic.	1	
			Any 3	3	
			Total	9	
4.4	36	(i)	1 Immunisation can be given through vaccination.	1	**CAS** page 16
			2 Vaccines are based on antigens that have been rendered harmless.	1	**HTP** page 184
			3 Dead/weakened/inactivated/parts of antigens used.	1	
			4 Adjuvants added to enhance the immune response.	1	
			5 Memory cells produced during the immune response.	1	
			6 Immunological memory created remains in the body for many years after the vaccination.	1	
			7 Produce more rapid/greater immune response following exposure to antigen.	1	
			Any 5	5	
		(ii)	8 Poverty prevents widespread vaccination.	1	
			9 Parental resistance to allowing their children to be vaccinated.	1	
			10 Malnutrition may make vaccination unsafe.	1	
			Any 2	2	
			Total	7	